CROSS STITCH
CARD COLLECTION

101 ORIGINAL DESIGNS

CLAIRE CROMPTON

David & Charles

Acknowledgments

I would like to thank the following suppliers for their generosity: DMC Creative World Ltd for supplying threads and Zweigart fabrics, and Impress Cards for the card mounts.

About the author

Claire Crompton studied knitwear design at college, and designed patterns for hand knitters. She then joined the design department of DMC where she worked on designs for kits and publications. Since she went freelance, Claire's designs have appeared in several cross stitching magazines, including *Cross Stitch Magic*. Her work has also appeared in books, and her designs feature in *Cross Stitch Greetings Cards* and *Cross Stitch Alphabets* published by David & Charles. Claire lives in the Tamar Valley, Cornwall.

A DAVID & CHARLES BOOK

First published in the UK in 2004

Text and designs Copyright © Claire Crompton 2004
Photography and layouts Copyright © David & Charles 2004

Distributed in North America
by F&W Publications, Inc.
4700 East Galbraith Road
Cincinnati, OH 45236
1-800-289-0963

A catalogue record for this book is available from the British Library.

ISBN 0 7153 1583 8

Visit our website at www.davidandcharles.co.uk

David & Charles books are available from all good bookshops; alternatively you can contact our Orderline on (0)1626 334555 or write to us at FREEPOST EX2 110, David & Charles Direct, Newton Abbot, TQ12 4ZZ (no stamp required UK mainland).

Printed in China by SNP Leefung
for David & Charles
Brunel House   Newton Abbot   Devon

Executive Editor Cheryl Brown
Desk Editor Jennifer Proverbs
Executive Art Editor Ali Myer
Designer Nigel Morgan
Production Controller Ros Napper

Contents

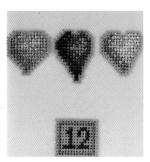

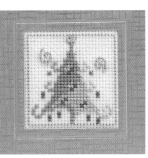

Introduction

*M*aking your own cards is not only pleasurable, *but it shows you care and ensures the perfect, tailor-made card for the recipient. But where do you begin and what do you do if time is short?*

HOW TO USE THIS BOOK

Your first step is to choose a design for your card. The cards are grouped by subject – Early Years, Growing Up, Greetings for Her, Greetings for Him, Special Sentiments and Card Giver's Calendar, which includes events such as Valentine's Day, Easter and Diwali. The card selector that opens each chapter shows all the cards featured to help you find what you are looking for at a glance. Simply choose your design, turn to the page indicated by the circled number to find the chart, and get stitching.

PERSONALIZING YOUR CARDS

The choice is vast and infinitely variable. For example, change the colour of the threads or the card mount, if desired, or choose another of the mounting methods featured. You can even alter the wording, changing a wedding card into a 'Get Well Soon' card, for example. There are also plenty of opportunities to personalize your card by adding a special message, the recipient's name, an important date or some other relevant detail. Using the alphabets, numbers and phrases on pages 96–98, it is easy to add the personal touch. Simply pencil the text onto the chart before you begin. Some cards have spaces left for this purpose with grey guidelines on the charts.

GETTING STARTED

All of the cards are straightforward and quite easy to stitch, using cross stitch and a few other basic stitches explained at the back of the book. But if you have hardly any time at all then take a look at the four 'Quick to Stitch' projects in every chapter that are super quick. Some have their own key, but others share their key with the main card, so you could even stitch them from left-over thread. I used DMC threads, but if you wish to use Anchor threads then refer to the conversion chart on page 104.

Be creative, be original and most of all send the right card!

Early Years

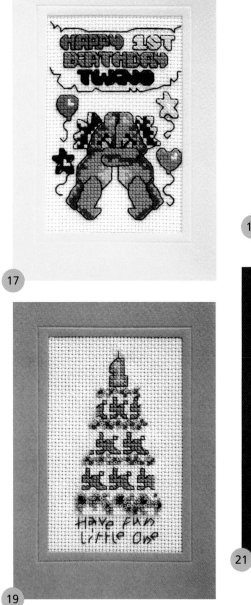

17

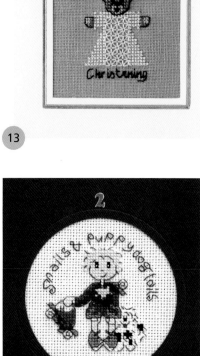

13

"It's Twins!"

9

19

21

8

12

10

Quick to Stitch

Birth Announcement

You will need

- 14 count cream Aida 12.5 x 12.5cm (5 x 5in)

- DMC stranded cotton (floss) as listed in the key

- 111 x 88mm (4⅜ x 3⅜in) plain card with deckle edge – Craft Creations Dec4U cream parchment

- Pink or blue ribbon bow

- Clear-drying glue

- Double-sided tape

Finished design size

5 x 5cm (2 x 2in)

To finish

Trim the fabric to within four rows of Aida on all sides. Fray the edges by carefully removing the outer row, then stick the design onto the card with double-sided tape. Add the ribbon bow using a small dab of glue

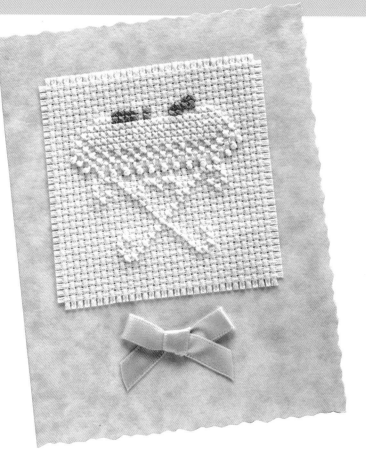

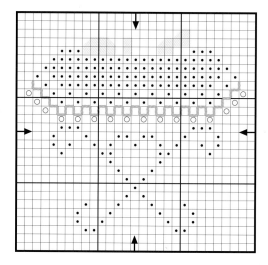

DMC stranded cotton cross stitch (use 2 strands)

	754
•	Blanc

french knots (use 2 strands)

○	Blanc

backstitch (use 2 strands)

〰〰	Blanc

It's Twins!

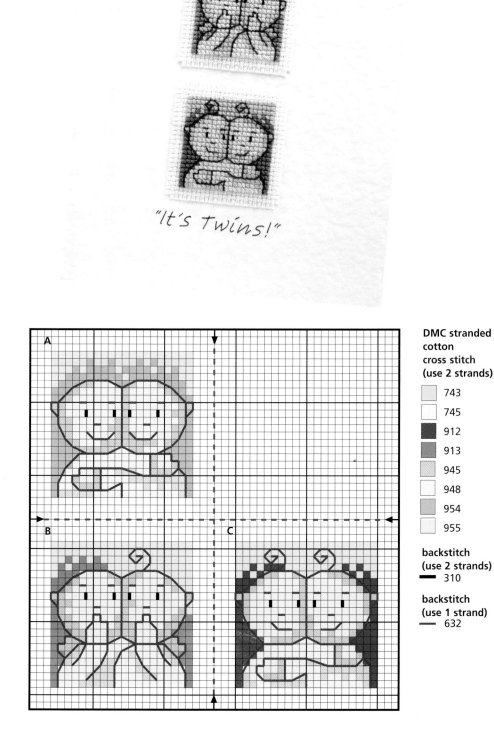

"It's Twins!"

You will need

- 16 count cream Aida
  18 x 18cm (7 x 7in)

- DMC stranded cotton
  (floss) as listed in the key

- 178 x 114mm (7 x 4½in)
  plain card – Craft Creations
  SF02U hammer cream

- Double-sided tape

Note
Stitch the three patches with
six squares of Aida between
them

Finished design size
Each patch is 3 x 3cm
(1¼in x 1¼in)

To finish
Separate the three patches
by carefully cutting between
them in the middle of the six
squares of Aida. Trim the
fabric on each patch to
within three rows of Aida on
the remaining sides. Fray the
edges by carefully removing
the outer row. Place the
patches onto the card in the
right order – A, B and C –
with approximately 5mm
(¼in) between them. Stick
each patch onto the card
using double-sided tape.
Write 'It's Twins!' beneath
the last patch

DMC stranded cotton
cross stitch
(use 2 strands)

- 743
- 745
- 912
- 913
- 945
- 948
- 954
- 955

backstitch
(use 2 strands)
— 310

backstitch
(use 1 strand)
— 632

New Baby Boy

You will need

- 16 count cream Aida
  15 x 15cm (6 x 6in)

- DMC stranded cotton
  (floss) as listed in the key

- 127 x 127mm (5 x 5in)
  card with 76 x 76mm
  (3 x 3in) aperture –
  Impress Cards T33 ivory
  felt 1x

Finished design size

7.5 x 7.5cm (3 x 3in)

Quick to Stitch

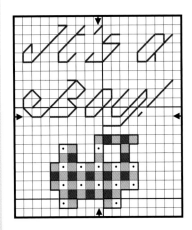

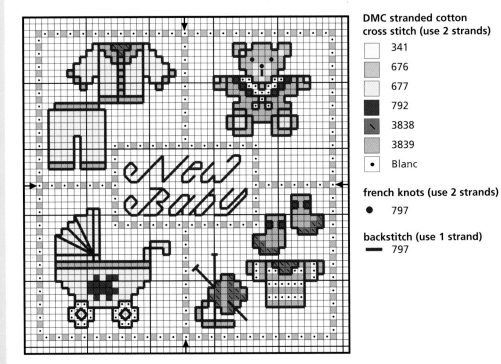

**DMC stranded cotton
cross stitch (use 2 strands)**

	341
	676
	677
	792
	3838
	3839
•	Blanc

french knots (use 2 strands)

●	797

backstitch (use 1 strand)

▬	797

New Baby Girl

You will need

- 16 count cream Aida
  15 x 15cm (6 x 6in)

- DMC stranded cotton
  (floss) as listed in the key

- 127 x 127mm (5 x 5in) card
  with 76 x 76mm (3 x 3in)
  aperture – Impress Cards
  T33 baby pink linen 08

Finished design size

7.5 x 7.5cm (3 x 3in)

DMC stranded cotton
cross stitch (use 2 strands)

	164
	676
	677
	961
/	963
	3716
•	Blanc

french knots (use 2 strands)

●	961

backstitch (use 1 strand)

—	335

Quick to Stitch

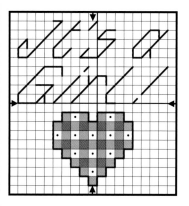

Christening Lamb

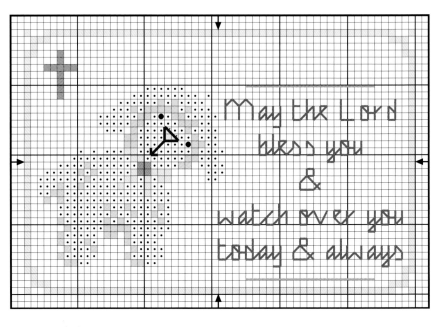

You will need

- 14 count cream Aida 15 x 18cm (6 x 7in)

- DMC stranded cotton (floss) and metallic thread as listed in the key

- 156 x 111mm (6¼ x 4⅜in) card with 111 x 72mm (4⅜ x 2⅞in) aperture – Impress Cards T24 silver linen 25

Note

To make this a landscape card, cut 7mm (¼in) off the bottom edge (the margin here is wider than it is at the top)

Finished design size

7 x 11cm (2¾ x 4⅜in)

Alternative colour

For a girl use 962 instead of 3839 and use 963 instead of 3840

Name

Add the child's name using the alphabet on page 96

**DMC stranded cotton
cross stitch (use 2 strands)**

▨	415	▨	3840 or 963
▨	963	•	Blanc
▨	3839 or 962	▨	5283 metallic

Backstitch (2 strands)
— 310

Backstitch (1 strand)
— 414
— 5283 metallic

French knots (2 strands)
● 310

Christening Teddy

You will need

- 28 count pink evenweave 20 x 17cm (8 x 6¾in)

- DMC stranded cotton (floss) as listed in the key

- 127 x 127mm (5 x 5in) card with 76 x 76mm (3 x 3in) aperture – Impress Cards T33 ivory 1x

- Silver pen

Note

Each stitch is worked over two threads of evenweave

Finished design size

6 x 5cm (2⅜ x 2in)

Alternative colour

For a boy use 28 count light blue evenweave

To finish

Work eyelet stitch for the front of the christening robe and pulled cross stitch on the arms and body of the robe following the instructions on pages 99 and 101. Fill in the impressed line around the aperture of the card with a silver pen

DMC stranded cotton
cross stitch (use 2 strands)
- 310
- 437
- 739

pulled cross stitch (use 2 strands)
- • Blanc

backstitch (use 2 strands)
- — 310

backstitch (use 1 strand)
- — 898

eyelet stitch (use 2 strands)
- ✳ Blanc

For New Grandparents

You will need

- 14 count white Aida 18 x 23cm (7 x 9in)

- DMC stranded cotton (floss) as listed in the key

- 178 x 114mm (7 x 4½in) plain card – Craft Creations SF02U lavender

Note

Stitch the two sections with four squares of Aida between them

Finished design size

9 x 14cm (3½ x 5½in)

Granddaughter

The design can be worked in pink for a girl: use DMC 3689 instead of 157, and DMC 3687 instead of 793. Stitch the outline of the Welcome patch, adding four more squares to the right side to make it 39 squares wide. Centralize the text – the chart for 'Granddaughter' is on page 96

To finish

Cut between the patches and trim the fabric on each patch to within two rows of Aida on all sides. Fray the edges by removing the outer row. Stick the patches onto the card with double-sided tape

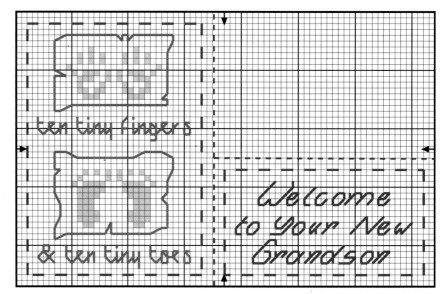

DMC stranded cotton cross stitch (use 2 strands)

▨	157 or 3689

backstitch (use 1 strand)

—	414
—	793 or 3687

First Christmas

You will need

- 28 count cream evenweave 15 x 15cm (6 x 6in)

- DMC stranded cotton (floss) as listed in the key

- 152 x 152mm (6 x 6in) card with 101 x 101mm (4 x 4in) aperture – Impress Cards T48 red linen 09

Note
Each stitch is worked over two threads

Finished design size
7.5 x 8.5cm (3 x 3⅜in)

DMC stranded cotton cross stitch (use 2 strands)

■	310		739	
	321		743	
	437	\	745	
	498		758	
	666		948	
	701	•	Blanc	
	703			

french knots (use 2 strands)
- ● 666
- ○ Blanc

backstitch (use 2 strands)
—— Blanc

backstitch (use 1 strand)
— 498
— 938

Quick to Stitch

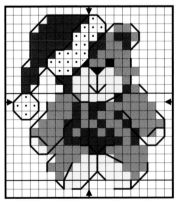

DMC stranded cotton cross stitch (use 2 strands)

	434
	436
	666
	739
	938
•	Blanc

backstitch (use 1 strand)
— 938

Christmas Baby

You will need

- 14 count cream Aida 20 x 18cm (8 x 7in)

- DMC stranded cotton (floss) as listed in the key

- 127 x 127mm (5 x 5in) card with 90mm (3½in) diameter aperture – Impress Cards T32 sky 3x

Finished design size

8 x 7cm (3¼ x 2¾in)

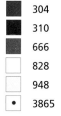

**DMC stranded cotton
cross stitch (use 2 strands)**

- 304
- 310
- 666
- 828
- 948
- • 3865

french knots (use 2 strands)

- ○ B5200

backstitch (use 2 strands)

- B5200

backstitch (use 1 strand)

- 413

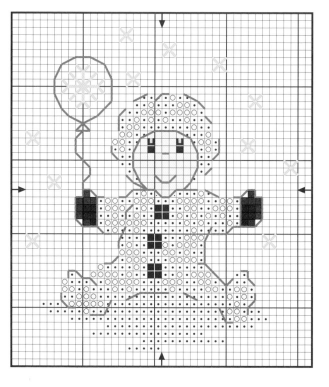

Twins' Birthday

You will need

- 14 count cream Aida
  18 x 13cm (7 x 5in)

- DMC stranded cotton
  (floss) as listed in the key

- 156 x 111mm (6¼ x 4⅜in)
  card with 111 x 72mm
  (4⅜ x 2¾in) aperture –
  Impress Cards T24
  sunflower 8x

Finished design size
10.5 x 5cm (4⅛ x 2in)

DMC stranded cotton
cross stitch (use 2 strands)

■	310
■	349
■	435
▧	437
▨	703
▨	722
□	727
□	739
•	Blanc

backstitch (use 2 strands)
— 310

backstitch (use 1 strand)
— 838

Boy's First Birthday

You will need

- 14 count cream Aida
  18 x 13cm (7 x 5in)

- DMC stranded cotton
  (floss) as listed in the key

- 156 x 111mm
  (6¼ x 4⅜in) card with
  111 x 72mm (4⅜ x 2¾in)
  aperture – Impress Cards
  T24 cobalt 2x

Finished design size

10.5 x 5cm (4⅛ x 2in)

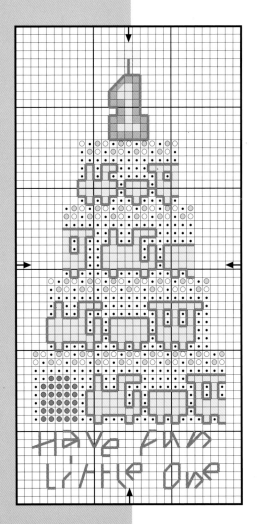

**DMC stranded cotton
cross stitch (use 2 strands)**

☐	3078
▨	3839
▨	3840
•	Blanc

french knots (use 2 strands)

○	415
●	840
○	Blanc

backstitch (use 1 strand)

—	3838

Girl's First Birthday

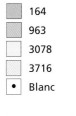

You will need

- 14 count cream Aida 18 x 13cm (7 x 5in)

- DMC stranded cotton (floss) as listed in the key

- 156 x 111mm (6¼ x 4⅜in) card with 111 x 72mm (4⅜ x 2¾in) aperture – Impress Cards T24 lilac 5x

Finished design size
10.5 x 5cm (4⅛ x 2in)

DMC stranded cotton cross stitch (use 2 strands)

▨	164
▨	963
☐	3078
▨	3716
•	Blanc

french knots (use 2 strands)

●	3687
●	3688
○	3689

backstitch (use 1 strand)

—	3687

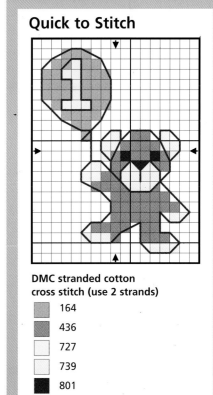

Quick to Stitch

DMC stranded cotton cross stitch (use 2 strands)

▨	164
▨	436
☐	727
☐	739
■	801

backstitch (use 1 strand)

—	801

Girl Two Today

You will need

- 16 count cream Aida 15 x 15cm (6 x 6in)

- DMC stranded cotton (floss) as listed in the key

- 127 x 127mm (5 x 5in) card with 90mm (3½in) diameter aperture – Impress Cards T32 lilac 5x

- Silver pen or Craft Creations self-adhesive stickers

Finished design size

6.5 x 6cm (2½ x 2⅜in)

To finish

Using self-adhesive stickers, add 'Happy Birthday' and '2' to the card mount. Alternatively, write on the details with a silver pen

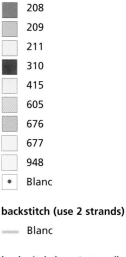

DMC stranded cotton
cross stitch (use 2 strands)

	208
	209
	211
	310
	415
	605
	676
	677
	948
•	Blanc

backstitch (use 2 strands)

— Blanc

backstitch (use 1 strand)

— 632

Boy Two Today

You will need

- 16 count cream Aida
  15 x 15cm (6 x 6in)

- DMC stranded cotton
  (floss) as listed in the key

- 156 x 111mm (6¼ x 4⅜in)
  card with 83mm (3¼in)
  diameter aperture –
  Impress Cards T21 cobalt 2x

- Silver pen or Craft
  Creations self-adhesive
  stickers

Finished design size
6.5 x 6.5cm (2½ x 2½in)

To finish
Using self-adhesive stickers,
add 'Happy Birthday' and '2'
to the card mount.
Alternatively, write on the
details with a silver pen

**DMC stranded cotton
cross stitch (use 2 strands)**

■	310
▨	350
▨	407
▨	677
▨	744
▨	798
▨	799
▨	817
▨	948
•	Blanc

backstitch (use 2 strands)
—— Blanc

backstitch (use 1 strand)
—— 632

Growing Up

33

29

27

32

25

31

well played!
congratulations!
great performance!

Quick to Stitch

30

26

27

24

28

29

31

26

Magical Birthday

You will need

- 32 count lilac evenweave 18 x 18cm (7 x 7in)

- DMC stranded cotton (floss) and metallic thread as listed in the key

- DMC V1 general beads as listed in the key

- 167 x 135mm (6½ x 5¼in) card with 95mm (3¾in) diameter aperture – Impress Cards T41 bright white linen 00

Note

Each stitch is worked over two threads

Finished design size

9 x 9cm (3½ x 3½in)

Name

Using 2 strands of 5288 and working in the spaces indicated by the grey line, add the child's age using the numbers on page 96

To finish

Write 'Have a Magical Birthday!' below the aperture

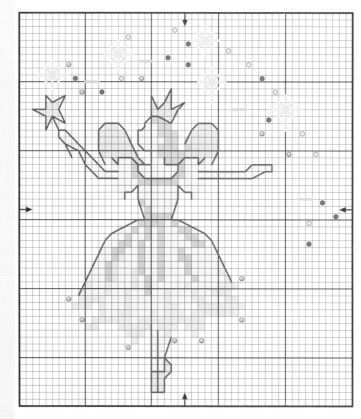

**DMC stranded cotton
cross stitch (use 2 strands)**

☐	775
☐	948
▨	3046
▨	3841

backstitch (use 1 strand)

—— 414

**DMC stranded metallic thread
cross stitch (use 2 strands)**

☐	5272

french knots (use 2 strands)

○ 5272
● 5288

backstitch (use 2 strands)

—— 5272
—— 5288

DMC beads

○ 10 Blanc

Alien Birthday

You will need
- 14 count navy Aida
  18 x 18cm (7 x 7in)

- DMC stranded cotton
  (floss) as listed in the key

- 152 x 152mm (6 x 6in) card
  with 101 x 101mm (4 x 4in)
  aperture – Impress Cards
  T48 silver linen 25

Finished design size
9 x 9cm (3½ x 3½in)

To personalize
In the space indicated by the
grey line add the number of
the child's birthday using the
numbers on page 96

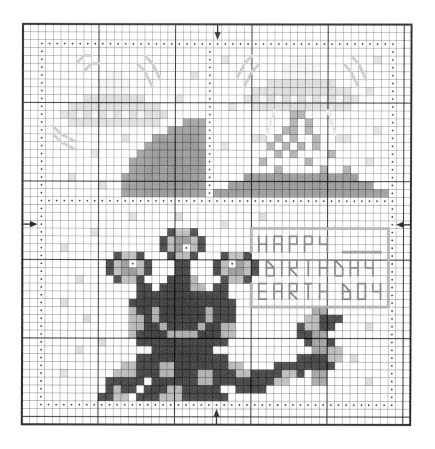

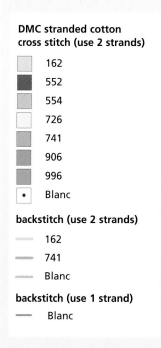

**DMC stranded cotton
cross stitch (use 2 strands)**

▨	162
■	552
▨	554
□	726
▨	741
▨	906
▨	996
•	Blanc

backstitch (use 2 strands)

⌇	162
—	741
—	Blanc

backstitch (use 1 strand)

—	Blanc

Babe

You will need

- 28 count mint evenweave 18 x 15cm (7 x 6in)

- DMC stranded cotton (floss) as listed in the key

- DMC V3 metallic beads as listed in the key

- 152 x 104mm (6 x 4⅛in) card with 114 x 70mm (4½ x 2¾in) aperture – Craft Creations AP08U raspberry

Note each stitch is worked over two threads

Finished design size

11.5 x 7cm (4½ x 2¾in)

Quick to Stitch

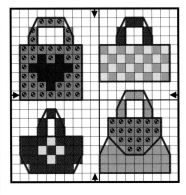

DMC stranded cotton
cross stitch (use 2 strands)

- 154
- 334
- 605
- 917
- 948
- 3325
- 3608
- 3835
- 3853

half cross stitch (use 2 strands)

- 165
- 166

backstitch (use 1 strand)

— 154
— 917

DMC beads

- 01 917
- 06 720

Dude

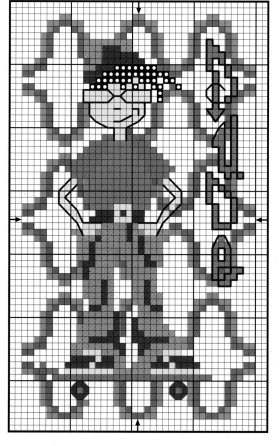

You will need

- 28 count apricot evenweave 18 x 15cm (7 x 6in)

- DMC stranded cotton (floss) as listed in the key

- 152 x 104mm (6 x 4⅛in) card with 114 x 70mm (4½ x 2¾in) aperture – Craft Creations AP08U lime green

Note each stitch is worked over two threads

Finished design size
11.5 x 7cm (4½ x 2¾in)

**DMC stranded cotton
cross stitch (use 2 strands)**

▨	150
◉	310
▨	703
▨	754
▨	3051
▨	3052
▨	3841
▨	3845

half cross stitch (use 2 strands)

▨	721
▨	722

backstitch (use 1 strand)

——	939

Quick to Stitch

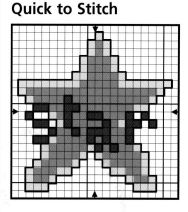

**DMC stranded cotton
cross stitch (use 2 strands)**

▨	150
▨	743
▨	970

backstitch (use 1 strand)

——	310

First Day at School

You will need

- 14 count white Aida 15 x 15cm (6 x 6in)

- DMC stranded cotton (floss) as listed in the key

- 127 x 127mm (5 x 5in) card with 76 x 76mm (3 x 3in) aperture – Impress Cards T33 ruby 7x

Finished design size
7.5 x 7.5cm (3 x 3in)

DMC stranded cotton cross stitch (use 2 strands)

■	336
■	347
□	745
■	798
■	905

backstitch (use 2 strands)

───	799

backstitch (use 1 strand)

───	318
───	552
───	798

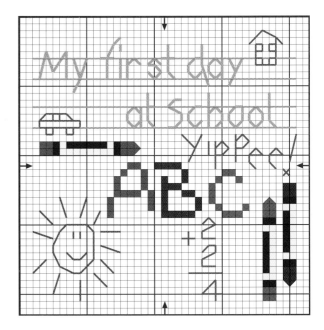

Music Exams

You will need

- 14 count cream Aida 15 x 15cm (6 x 6in)

- DMC stranded cotton (floss) as listed in the key

- 127 x 127mm (5 x 5in) card with 76 x 76mm (3 x 3in) aperture – Impress Cards T33 ivory 1x

Finished design size

7.5 x 7cm (3 x 2¾in)

Note

Work the lines of music before the notes

To finish

Photocopy or use old sheet music and cut four strips to fit around the aperture. Attach with double-sided tape

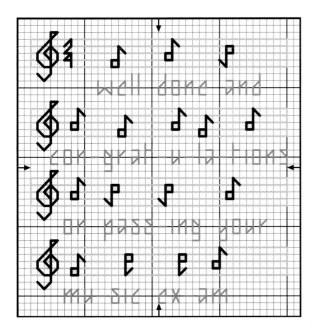

**DMC stranded cotton
cross stitch (use 2 strands)**

☐ 310

backstitch (use 2 strands)

━ 310

backstitch (use 1 strand)

┈ 318
── 413

Quick to Stitch

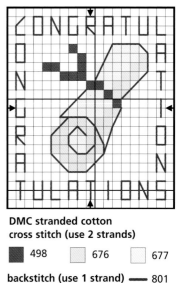

**DMC stranded cotton
cross stitch (use 2 strands)**

■ 498   ☐ 676   ☐ 677

backstitch (use 1 strand) ━ 801

Football Pennant

You will need

- 16 count cream Aida
  15 x 13cm (6 x 5in)

- DMC stranded cotton
  (floss) as listed in the key
  and DMC perlé 5 thread,
  shade 676 for a fringe

- Cream backing fabric
  15 x 13cm (6 x 5in)

- 178 x 114mm (7 x 4½in)
  plain card – Craft Creations
  SF02U bright red

Finished pennant size

12 x 10cm (4¾ x 4in)

To finish

Mark the centre of the
bottom edge, then mark
2cm (¾in) up on each side.
Draw a line from each
mark to the centre point
and cut. Lay the design
face down on the backing
fabric, tack and trim to
match. Stitch along the
sides and shaped edges
with a 1.5cm (⅝in) seam,
leaving the top edge open.
Trim the seams and turn
out; press. Turn in the raw
edge at the top and tack.
Topstitch around the
pennant. Add a perlé
thread fringe and twisted
cord following the
instructions on page 101.
Stick to the card with
double-sided tape

DMC stranded cotton
cross stitch (use 2 strands)

■	304
◉	310
▨	318
■	666
□	948
•	Blanc

backstitch (use 1 strand)
—— 310

To personalize

Add a favourite team's name
using the alphabet on page 96;
use the team colours for the
football kit

Number 1

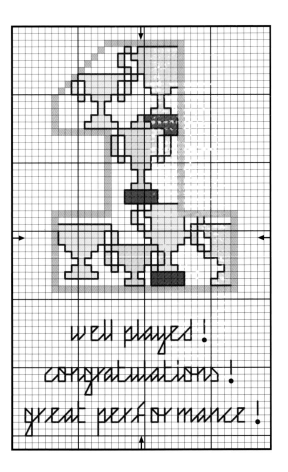

You will need

- 16 count antique white
  Aida 18 x 15cm (7 x 6in)

- DMC stranded cotton
  (floss) as listed in the key

- 178 x 114mm (7 x 4½in)
  plain card – Craft Creations
  SF02U plasma blue

Finished design size

10 x 6cm (4 x 2⅜in)

To finish

Cut apart the number and
the words. Trim the fabric all
around each piece to within
two rows of Aida. Attach the
number and words as shown
using double-sided tape

**DMC stranded cotton
cross stitch (use 2 strands)**

 317
415

french knots (use 1 strand)

● 823

backstitch (use 1 strand)

— 823

**DMC stranded metallic thread
cross stitch (use 2 strands)**

5282
5283

Quick to Stitch

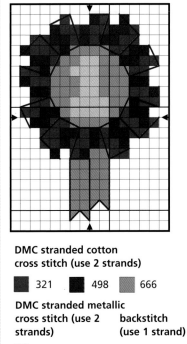

**DMC stranded cotton
cross stitch (use 2 strands)**

| 321 | 498 | 666 |

**DMC stranded metallic
cross stitch (use 2
strands)** | | **backstitch
(use 1 strand)**

5282 | — 938

First Holy Communion

You will need

- 14 count white Aida 18 x 15cm (7 x 6in)

- DMC stranded cotton (floss) as listed in the key plus 414 to personalize the card

- 156 x 111mm (6 x 4⅜in) card with 111 x 72mm (4⅜ x 2⅞in) aperture – Impress Cards T24 ivory 1x

Finished design size

10.5 x 7cm (4⅛ x 2¾in)

To personalize

Add the child's name and the date with 1 strand of DMC stranded cotton 414 using the alphabet and numbers on page 96 and following the grey lines as a guide

**DMC stranded cotton
cross stitch (use 2 strands)**

	151
	498
	676
	677
	729
	3348
	3733

backstitch (use 1 strand)

—	729

**DMC stranded metallic thread
cross stitch (use 2 strands)**

	5283

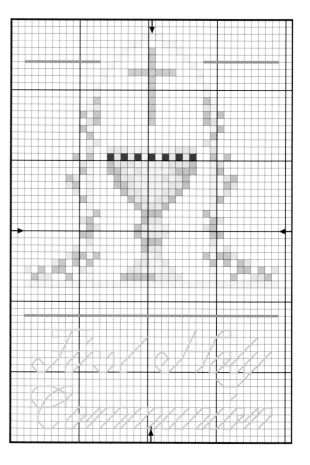
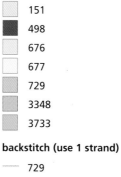

Bar Mitzvah

You will need

- 14 count cream Aida 15 x 15cm (6 x 6in)

- DMC stranded cotton (floss) as listed in the key

- 152 x 104mm (6 x 4⅛in) card with 82 x 79mm (3¼ x 3⅛in) aperture – Craft Creations AP10U dark blue

Finished design size
7.5 x 7.5cm (3 x 3in)

For a girl
Work 'Bat Mitzvah' using the chart on page 96

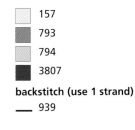

DMC stranded cotton
cross stitch (use 2 strands)

▢	157
▨	793
▨	794
▦	3807

backstitch (use 1 strand)

— 939

Greetings For Her

49

38

45

36

42

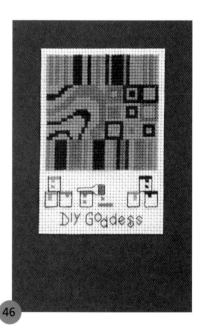

46

37

39

44

Quick to Stitch

43

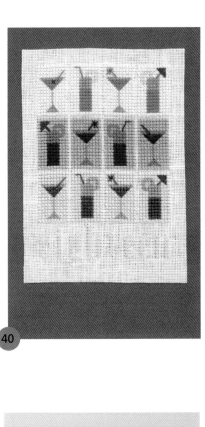

40

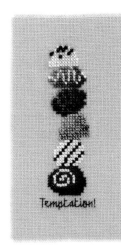

48

41

47

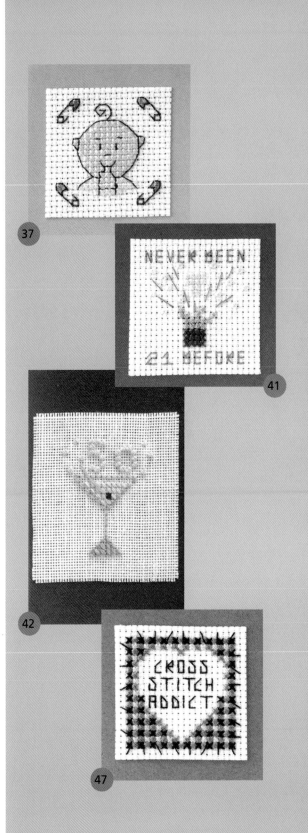

37

41

42

47

Mother's Day

You will need

- 32 count light blue evenweave 18 x 18cm (7 x 7in)

- DMC stranded cotton (floss) as listed in the key

- 167 X 135mm (6½ x 5¼in) card with 95mm (3¾in) diameter aperture – Impress Cards T41 palest blue 03

Note

Each stitch is worked over two threads of evenweave

Finished design size

9 x 9cm (3½ x 3½in)

DMC stranded cotton cross stitch (use 2 strands)

☐	369
▨	562
☐	564
▨	3839

french knots (use 2 strands)

●	209
○	211
○	3823

backstitch (use 1 strand)

—	3807

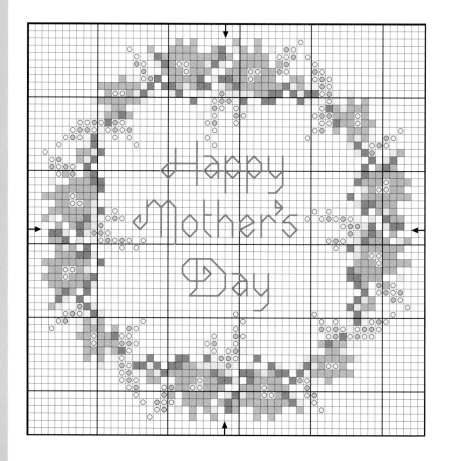

New Mum

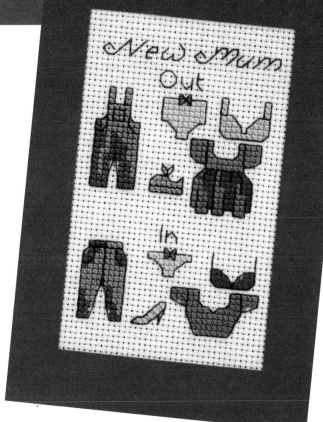

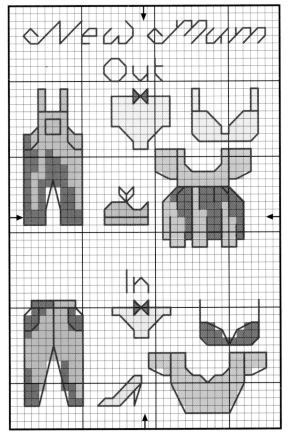

You will need

- 14 count white Aida
  20 x 16.5cm (8 x 6½in)

- DMC stranded cotton
  (floss) as listed in the key

- 152 x 104mm (6 x 4⅛in)
  card with 114 x 70mm
  (4½ x 2¾in) aperture – Craft
  Creations AP08U raspberry

Finished design size

9.5 x 6.5cm (3¾ x 2½in)

DMC stranded cotton
cross stitch (use 2 strands)

	211
	603
	605
	813
	826
	3747

backstitch (use 1 strand)

— 632

Quick to Stitch

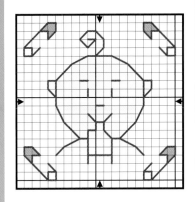

DMC stranded cotton
cross stitch (use 2 strands)

	340
	727
	951

backstitch (use 1 strand)

— 632

Happy Birthday

You will need

- 14 count white Aida
  18 x 20cm (7 x 8in)

- DMC stranded cotton
  (floss) as listed in the key

- Mill Hill beads as listed
  in the key

- 104 x 152mm (4⅛ x 6in)
  card with 70 x 114mm
  (2¾ x 4½in) aperture –
  Craft Creations AP08U
  violet

Finished design size
7 x 10cm (2¾ x 4in)

**DMC stranded cotton
cross stitch (use 2 strands)**

■ 3837

backstitch (use 2 strands)
— 3837

backstitch (use 1 strand)
— 208
— 209

frosted glass beads
○ 62047

Mackintosh Rose

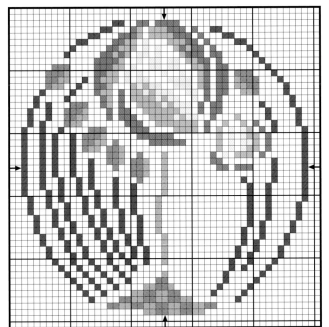

You will need

- 14 count white Aida
  18 x 18cm (7 x 7in)

- DMC stranded cotton
  (floss) as listed in the key

- 167 x 135mm (6½ x 5¼in)
  card with 95mm (3¾in)
  diameter aperture –
  Impress Cards T41 baby
  pink 08

- Double-sided tape

Finished design size
9 x 9cm (3½ x 3½in)

To finish
Work 'Happy Birthday' on a small piece of 14 count white Aida. Trim the fabric to within four rows of the Aida on all sides, then fray the edges by carefully removing the outer row. Stick the words onto the card under the aperture with double-sided tape

**DMC stranded cotton
cross stitch
(use 2 strands)**

- 905
- 906
- 907
- 962
- 963
- 3716

backstitch (use 1 strand)

- 962

Eighteen

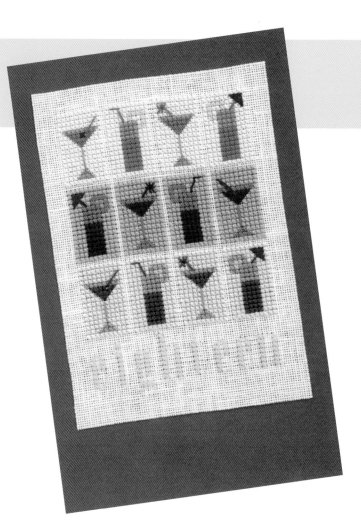

You will need

- 28 count white evenweave 21.5 x 18cm (8½ x 7in)

- DMC stranded cotton (floss) as listed in the key

- 178 x 114mm (7 x 4½in) plain card – Craft Creations SF02U raspberry

- Double-sided tape

Note

Each stitch is worked over two threads of evenweave

Finished design size

11.5 x 8cm (4½ x 3⅛in)

To finish

Trim the fabric to within 1cm (⅜in) of the finished design and then use double-sided tape to attach the design to the card

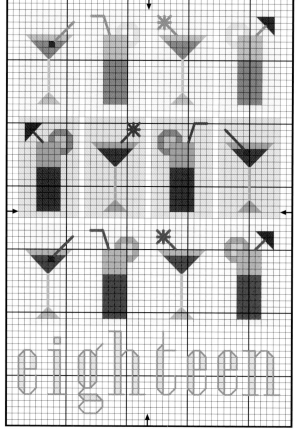

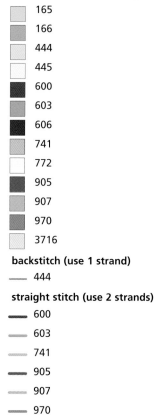

DMC stranded cotton cross stitch (use 2 strands)

	165
	166
	444
	445
	600
	603
	606
	741
	772
	905
	907
	970
	3716

backstitch (use 1 strand)

——	444

straight stitch (use 2 strands)

——	600
——	603
——	741
——	905
——	907
——	970

21 Today

You will need

- 14 count antique white Aida 20 x 15cm (8 x 6in)

- DMC stranded cotton (floss) and metallic thread as listed in the key

- 152 x 104mm (6 x 4⅛in) card with 114 x 70mm (4½ x 2¾in) aperture – Craft Creations AP08M silver

Finished design size
10 x 5cm (4 x 2in)

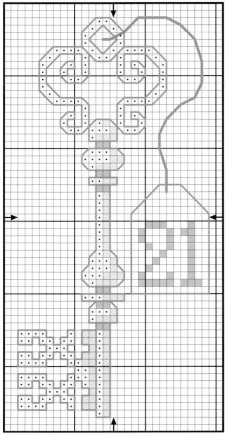

DMC stranded cotton cross stitch (use 2 strands)

- 318
- 415
- • 762

backstitch (use 2 strands)
— 414

backstitch (use 1 strand)
— 414

DMC stranded metallic thread cross stitch (use 2 strands)

- 5283

Quick to Stitch

DMC stranded cotton cross stitch (use 2 strands)

- 699
- 746

french knots (use 2 strands)
- ○ 746

backstitch (use 1 strand)
— 420

DMC stranded metallic thread cross stitch (use 2 strands)

- 5282

Fifty

You will need

- 28 count white evenweave 20 x 20cm (8 x 8in)

- DMC stranded cotton (floss) and metallic thread as listed in the key

- 203 x 150mm (8 x 6in) card with 145 x 94mm (5¾ x 3¾in) aperture – Craft Creations AP02M gold

Note

Each stitch is worked over two threads of evenweave

Finished design size

11 x 8cm (4¼ x 3⅛in)

Quick to Stitch

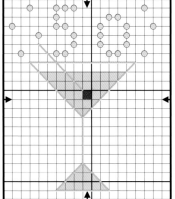

DMC stranded cotton
cross stitch (use 2 strands)

- 304
- 3855

french knots (use 2 strands)
- ⬤ 3855

backstitch (use 1 strand)
- —— 3854

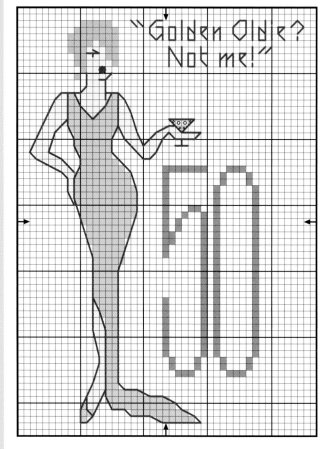

DMC stranded cotton
cross stitch (use 2 strands)

- ■ 304
- ▨ 422
- ⊙ 677
- □ 948

backstitch (use 1 strand)

- —— 632

DMC stranded metallic thread
cross stitch (use 2 strands)

- 5282

DMC stranded cotton with DMC
stranded metallic thread
cross stitch (use 1 strand of
each colour)

- 422 + 5282

Sixty

You will need

• 28 count white evenweave 22 x 18cm (8¾ x 7in)

• DMC stranded cotton (floss) and metallic thread as listed in the key

• Mill Hill beads as listed in the key

• 203 x 150mm (8 x 6in) card with 145 x 94mm (5¾ x 3¾in) aperture – Craft Creations AP02M silver

Note

Each stitch is worked over two threads of evenweave

Finished design size

12 x 7cm (4¾ x 2¾in)

**DMC stranded cotton
cross stitch (use 2 strands)**

■ 304

■ 310

○ 677

□ 948

backstitch (use 1 strand)

— 413

**DMC stranded metallic thread
cross stitch (use 2 strands)**

▨ 5283

**DMC stranded cotton with DMC
stranded metallic thread
cross stitch (use 1 strand of
each colour)**

▨ 415 + 5283

glass seed beads

○ 00161

Born to Shop

You will need

- 16 count pink Aida
  15 x 20cm (6 x 8in)

- DMC stranded cotton
  (floss) as listed in the key

- 104 x 152mm (4⅛ x 6in)
  card with 70 x 114mm
  (2¾ x 4½in) aperture –
  Craft Creations AP08U
  raspberry

Finished design size

5.5 x 11cm (2¼ x 4¼in)

To personalize

Use the alphabet and
words from page 97 to add
your own message
following the grey line as a
guide. Work the letters in
backstitch using one strand
of 600

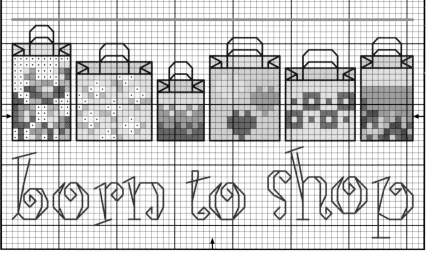

**DMC stranded cotton
cross stitch (use 2 strands)**

■	208
■	209
▨	211
▨	602
▨	603
▨	605
▨	702
▨	704
□	745
▨	3840
•	Blanc

backstitch (use 1 strand)

——	550
——	600

Domestic Goddess

You will need

- 16 count pink Aida 20 x 15cm (8 x 6in)

- DMC stranded cotton (floss) as listed in the key

- 152 x 104mm (6 x 4⅛in) card with 114 x 70mm (4½ x 2¾in) aperture – Craft Creations AP08U raspberry

Finished design size
10.5 x 6.5cm (4⅛ x 2½in)

To personalize
Use the alphabet and words from page 97 to add your own message following the grey lines as a guide. Work in backstitch using one strand of 603

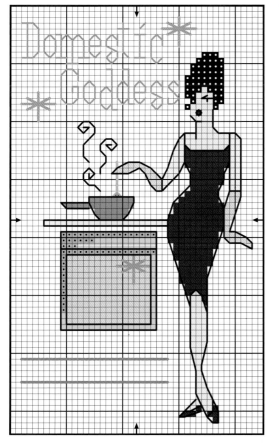

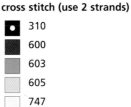

DMC stranded cotton cross stitch (use 2 strands)

⬛	310
⬛	600
▨	603
▨	605
☐	747
☐	948
•	959
▨	964

backstitch (use 2 strands)

——	959
——	Blanc

backstitch (use 1 strand)

——	310
——	603

DIY Goddess

You will need

- 14 count cream Aida 20 x 18cm (8 x 7in)

- DMC stranded cotton (floss) as listed in the key

- 178 x 114mm (7 x 4½in) plain card – Craft Creations SF02U violet

- Double-sided tape

Finished design size
10.5 x 7cm (4⅛ x 2¾in)

To personalize
Use the alphabet and words from page 97 to add your own message in place of 'DIY Goddess'. Work in backstitch using one strand of 3837

To finish
Trim the fabric to within two rows of Aida on all sides. Stick the design onto the card using double-sided tape

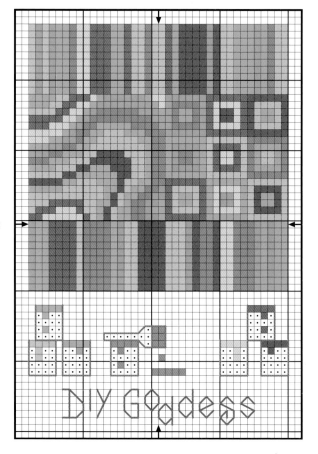

DMC stranded cotton
cross stitch (use 2 strands)

	704
	718
	894
	3340
	3806
	3837
	3846
•	Blanc

backstitch (use 1 strand)

——	718
——	3837

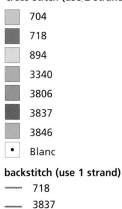

Cross Stitch Addict

You will need

- 14 count cream Aida 20 x 18cm (8 x 7in)

- DMC stranded cotton (floss) as listed in the key

- 156 x 111mm (6¼ x 4⅜in) card with 111 x 72mm (4⅜ x 2⅞in) aperture – Impress Cards T24 lavender 07

Finished design size

11 x 7cm (4¼ x 2¾in)

To personalize

Use the alphabet and words from page 97 to add your own message in place of the motto. Work in backstitch using one strand of 221

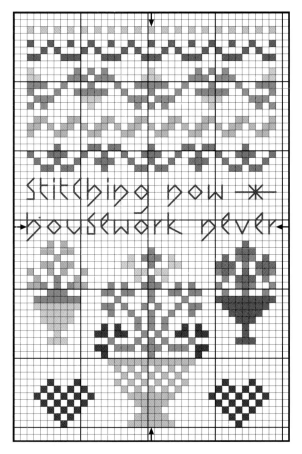

DMC stranded cotton cross stitch (use 2 strands)

▨	161
▨	221
▨	223
▨	224
▨	340
▨	729
▨	3816
▨	3835

backstitch (use 1 strand)
— 221

Quick to Stitch

DMC stranded cotton cross stitch (use 2 strands)

▨	153
■	550
▨	553

backstitch (use 1 strand)
— 550

Chocoholic

You will need

- 28 count lilac evenweave
  20 x 15cm (8 x 6in)

- DMC stranded cotton
  (floss) and metallic
  thread as listed in
  the key

- Mill Hill beads as listed in
  the key

- 178 x 114mm (7 x 4½in)
  plain card – Craft
  Creations SF02U
  hammer cream

- Double-sided tape

Note

Each stitch is worked over
two threads of evenweave

Finished design size

10 x 4cm (4 x 1½in)

To personalize

Use the alphabet and
words from page 97 to add
your own message in place
of 'Temptation'. Work in
backstitch using one strand
of 898

To finish

Trim the fabric to within
2cm (¾in) of the finished
design. Fray the edges by
carefully removing the
outer row. Stick the design
onto the card using
double-sided tape

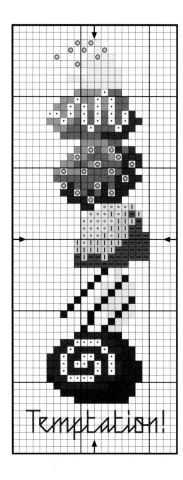

**DMC stranded cotton
cross stitch (use 2 strands)**

■	632
☐	712
■	898
▨	3064
▨	3772
☐	3865

backstitch (use 1 strand)
— 898

**DMC stranded cotton with DMC
stranded metallic thread
cross stitch (use 1 strand of each)**

○	3064 + 5272
I	3772 + 5272
▬	632 + 5272
·	3865 + 5272

antique glass beads

◉	03024

Good Intentions

You will need
- 28 count lilac evenweave 15 x 15cm (6 x 6in)

- DMC stranded cotton (floss) as listed in the key

- 127 x 127mm (5 x 5in) card with 76 x 76mm (3 x 3in) aperture – Impress Cards T33 chocolate 9x

Note
Each stitch is worked over two threads of evenweave

Finished design size
6 x 5.5cm (2⅜ x 2¼in)

To personalize
Use the alphabet and words from page 97 to add your own message in place of this one. Work in backstitch using one strand of 898

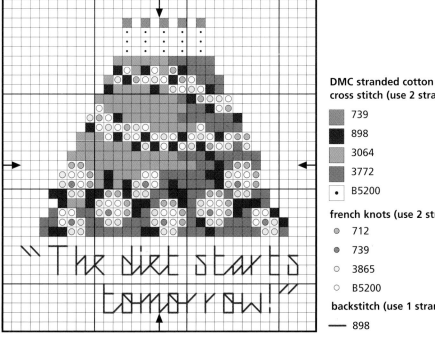

DMC stranded cotton cross stitch (use 2 strands)

▨	739
■	898
▨	3064
▨	3772
·	B5200

french knots (use 2 strands)

●	712
●	739
○	3865
○	B5200

backstitch (use 1 strand)

——	898

Greetings For Him

40-Not Out!

59

Catch a Wave!

Happy 18th Bday!

Surf's Up!

55

Happy Father's Day, Dad

52

Retirement - a full time gardening job!

57

Driving to The 19th Hole

60

GOAL!

CORNER

"Football crazy
Football mad!"

58

For my
Domestic God!

63

FOR SALE

NEW DAD

53

Quick to Stitch

Father's Day

You will need

- 28 count antique white evenweave 18 x 18cm (7 x 7in)

- DMC stranded cotton (floss) as listed in the key

- 152 x 104mm (6 x 4⅛in) card with 83mm (3¼in) diameter aperture – Craft Creations AP09U pale blue

Note

Each stitch is worked over two threads of evenweave

Finished design size

7 x 7cm (2¾ x 2¾in)

To finish

Write 'Happy Father's Day, Dad' beneath the aperture

Quick to Stitch

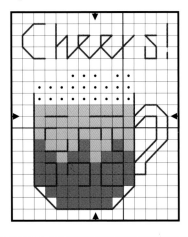

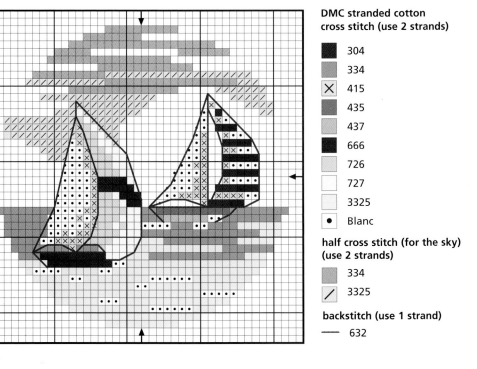

DMC stranded cotton
cross stitch (use 2 strands)

■	304
▨	334
☒	415
▨	435
▨	437
■	666
☐	726
☐	727
☐	3325
•	Blanc

half cross stitch (for the sky)
(use 2 strands)

▨	334
⁄	3325

backstitch (use 1 strand)

—	632

New Dad

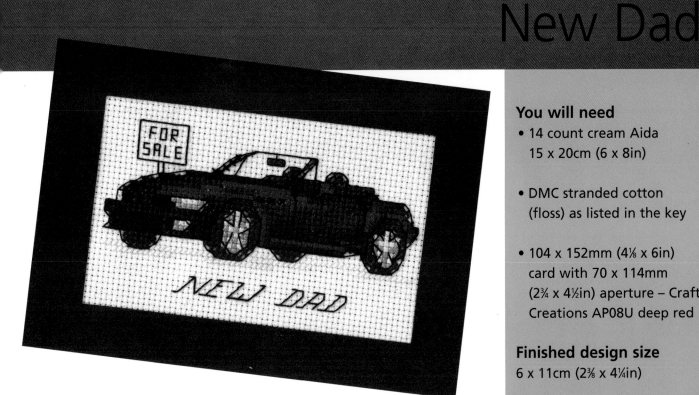

You will need

- 14 count cream Aida
  15 x 20cm (6 x 8in)

- DMC stranded cotton
  (floss) as listed in the key

- 104 x 152mm (4⅛ x 6in)
  card with 70 x 114mm
  (2¾ x 4½in) aperture – Craft
  Creations AP08U deep red

Finished design size
6 x 11cm (2⅜ x 4¼in)

DMC stranded cotton
cross stitch (use 2 strands)

▨	304
▨	318
▨	321
☐	762
■	814
▨	3799
▨	3801

half cross stitch (use 2 strands)

☐	762

backstitch (use 1 strand)

— 310

Quick to Stitch

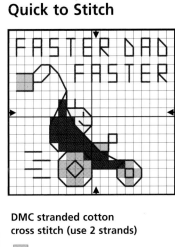

DMC stranded cotton
cross stitch (use 2 strands)

▨	164
■	304
▨	318
☐	951

backstitch (use 1 strand)

— 938

Happy Birthday

You will need

- 16 count cream Aida
  15 x 20cm (6 x 8in)

- DMC stranded cotton
  (floss) as listed in the key

- 104 x 152mm (4⅛ x 6in)
  card with 70 x 114mm
  (2¾ x 4½in) aperture –
  Craft Creations AP08U
  deep green

Finished design size

6 x 10cm (2⅜ x 4in)

DMC stranded cotton
cross stitch (use 2 strands)

▨	163
▨	221

backstitch (use 1 strand)

— 319

— 902 (around each letter)

french knots (use 2 strands)

● 902

18th Birthday

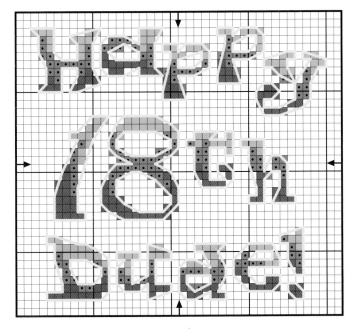

To finish

To create the surfboard shape, cut thin white card 17.5 x 8.5cm (7 x 3⅜in). Mark the centre of one short end then measure 6cm (2⅜in) up each side from this end and mark. Draw a curve from each mark to the centre to make a pointed end. At the other end do the same but only 2.5cm (1in) from the end. Cut out the surfboard, draw round it onto white card, then cut out 0.5cm (¼in) inside the pencil line.

Now place the first, larger surfboard onto the wrong side of the fabric to cover the stitching and draw round it. Cut out the fabric 2.5cm (1in) outside the line. Stick double-sided tape along the edges of the card and lay it tape-side up on the wrong side of the fabric. Turn back the excess fabric, sticking it to the tape. Using PVA glue or more tape, stick the smaller surfboard onto the back, covering the fabric's raw edges.

To finish the card, stick the surfboard onto the silver card with tape

You will need

- 14 count waste canvas 20 x 20cm (8 x 8in)

- Blue printed cotton with wave pattern or tie-dye effect 30 x 20cm (12 x 8in)

- DMC stranded cotton (floss) as listed in the key

- 144 x 144mm (5⅝ x 5⅝in) plain card – Craft Creations SF06M silver

- PVA and double-sided tape

- Pen to write your wording on the card (optional)

Note

Work the design on waste canvas over the blue fabric and then tease away the threads of canvas to leave the stitching on the cotton. See Stitching Techniques, page 101 for further details on using waste canvas

Finished design size

8 x 8cm (3⅛ x 3⅛in)

DMC stranded cotton
cross stitch (use 2 strands)

741

946

970

backstitch (use 2 strands)

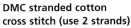

725

21st Football Shirt

You will need
- 14 count white Aida
  15 x 18cm (6 x 7in)

- DMC stranded cotton
  (floss) as listed in the key

- 152 x 104mm (6 x 4⅛in)
  card with 82 x 79mm
  (3¼ x 3⅛in) aperture –
  Craft Creations
  AP10M gold

Finished design size
7 x 5.5cm (2¾ x 2¼in)

Note
Work three-quarter
stitches on the numbers in
Blanc and the remaining
quarter stitches in 3325
(see page 99)

To personalize
Stitch the shirt in a
favourite team's colours

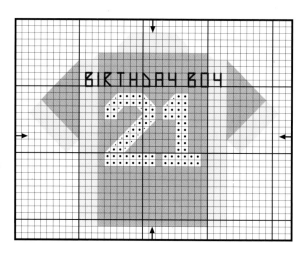

**DMC stranded cotton
cross stitch (use 2 strands)**

	775
	3325
•	Blanc

backstitch (use 1 strand)
— 336

Gardening

You will need

- 14 count pale green Aida 18 x 18cm (7 x 7in)

- DMC stranded cotton (floss) as listed in the key

- 144 x 144mm (5⅝ x 5⅝in) card with 96 x 96mm (3¾ x 3¾in) aperture – Craft Creations AP08U dark brown

Finished design size

9 x 9cm (3½ x 3½in)

To personalize

Referring to the alphabet and words on page 98, write your own message onto the chart following the grey lines as a guide. Work in backstitch, using one strand of 801

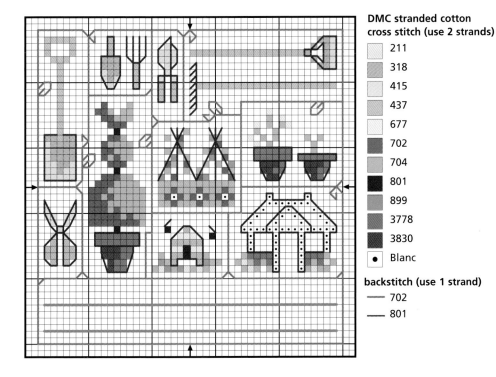

DMC stranded cotton
cross stitch (use 2 strands)

	211
	318
	415
	437
	677
	702
	704
	801
	899
	3778
	3830
•	Blanc

backstitch (use 1 strand)

— 702
— 801

Quick to Stitch

Football Crazy

You will need

- 14 count mint green Aida 20 x 18cm (8 x 7in)

- DMC stranded cotton (floss) as listed in the key

- 156 x 111mm (6⅛ x 4⅜in) card with 111 x 72mm (4⅜ x 2⅞in) aperture – Impress Cards T24 chalk 0x

Finished design size

10.5 x 7cm (4⅛ x 2¾in)

To personalize

Use the alphabet and words from page 98 to add your own message in place of the one given

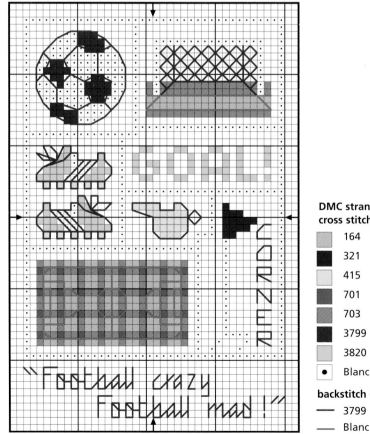

Quick to Stitch

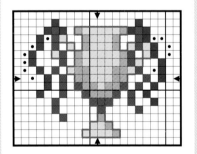

DMC stranded cotton cross stitch (use 2 strands)

■	317
■	318
□	415
■	666
■	792
•	Blanc

backstitch (use 1 strand)

— 317

DMC stranded cotton cross stitch (use 2 strands)

■	164
■	321
■	415
■	701
■	703
■	3799
■	3820
•	Blanc

backstitch (use 1 strand)

— 3799

— Blanc

Cricket

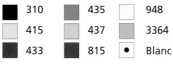

You will need

- 16 count cream Aida
  15 x 20cm (6 x 8in)

- DMC stranded cotton
  (floss) as listed in the key

- 156 x 111mm (6¼ x 4⅜in)
  card with 111 x 72mm
  (4⅜ x 2⅞in) aperture –
  Impress Cards T24 soft
  green 06

Note

To make this into a
landscape card, cut 7mm
(¼in) off the bottom edge
(the margin here is wider
than at the top)

Finished design size

5.5 x 10cm (2¼ x 4in)

To personalize

Use the alphabet and words
from page 98 to add your
own message to the card
following the grey line as a
guide. Work in backstitch,
using one strand of 433

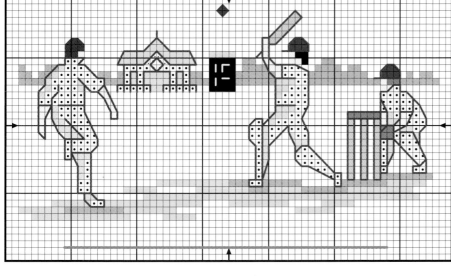

**DMC stranded cotton
cross stitch (use 2 strands)**

■ 310	435	948
415	437	3364
433	815	• Blanc

**half cross stitch
(use 2 strands)**

3348

**backstitch
(use 1 strand)**

— 433
Blanc

Golf

You will need

- 16 count cream Aida 18 x 18cm (7 x 7in)

- DMC stranded cotton (floss) as listed in the key

- 152 x 104mm (6 x 4⅛in) card with 82 x 79mm (3¼ x 3⅛in) aperture – Craft Creations AP10U black

Finished design size
7.5 x 7.5cm (3 x 3in)

To personalize
Use the alphabet and words from page 98 to add your own message to the card, following the grey line as a guide. Work in backstitch using one strand of 310

DMC stranded cotton cross stitch (use 2 strands)

 310

half cross stitch (use 2 strands)

	931
	932
	945
	3752

backstitch (use 1 strand)

—— 310

Gone Fishing

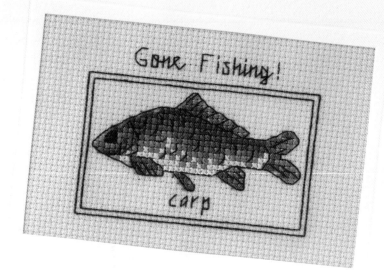

You will need

- 14 count ecru Aida
  15 x 20cm (6 x 8in)

- DMC stranded cotton
  (floss) as listed in the key

- 156 x 111mm (6¼ x 4⅜in)
  card with 111 x 72mm
  (4⅜ x 2⅞in) aperture –
  Impress Cards T24 ivory 1x

Note

To make this into a
landscape card, cut 7mm
(¼in) off the bottom edge
(the margin here is wider
than at the top)

Finished design size

5.5 x 8cm (2¼ x 3¼in)

To personalize

Use the alphabet and words
from page 98 to add your
own message to the card
following the grey line as a
guide. Work in backstitch,
using one strand of 839

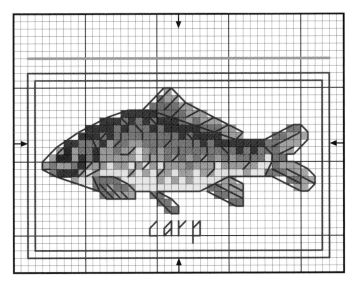

**DMC stranded cotton
cross stitch (use 2 strands)**

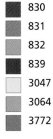

- 830
- 831
- 832
- 839
- 3047
- 3064
- 3772

backstitch (use 1 strand)
——— 839

DIY

You will need

- 14 count cream Aida 23 x 13cm (9 x 5in)

- DMC stranded cotton (floss) as listed in the key

- 152 x 104mm (6 x 4⅛in) plain card – Craft Creations SF03U dark blue

- Double-sided tape

Finished design size
13.5 x 3.5cm (5¼ x 1½in)

To personalize
Use the alphabet and words from page 98 to add your own message to the card, following the grey lines as a guide. Work in backstitch, using one strand of 413

To finish
Trim the fabric to within four rows of the Aida on all sides. Fray the edges by carefully removing the outer row, then stick the design onto the card with double-sided tape

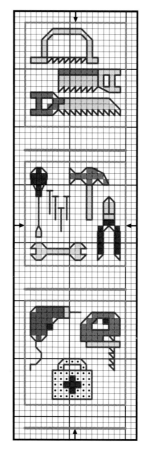

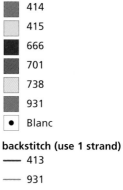

**DMC stranded cotton
cross stitch (use 2 strands)**

▨	414
▨	415
▨	666
▨	701
▨	738
▨	931
•	Blanc

backstitch (use 1 strand)

——	413
——	931

Barbecue

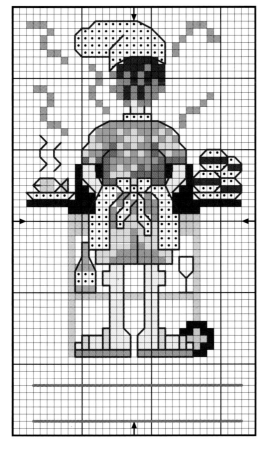

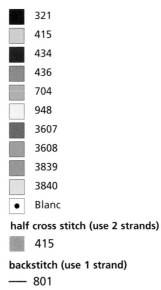

You will need
- 14 count cream Aida
  20 x 15cm (8 x 6in)

- DMC stranded cotton
  (floss) as listed in the key

- 152 x 104mm (6 x 4⅛in)
  card with 114 x 70mm
  (4½ x 2¾in) aperture – Craft
  Creations AP08U lavender

Finished design size
10.5 x 6cm (4⅛ x 2⅜in)

To personalize
Use the alphabet and words
from page 98 to add your
own message to the card,
following the grey lines as a
guide. Work in backstitch,
using one strand of 801

DMC stranded cotton
cross stitch (use 2 strands)

■	321
▨	415
■	434
▨	436
▨	704
□	948
▨	3607
▨	3608
▨	3839
▨	3840
•	Blanc

half cross stitch (use 2 strands)

▨	415

backstitch (use 1 strand)

—	801

Special Sentiments

78

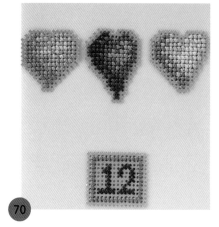

70

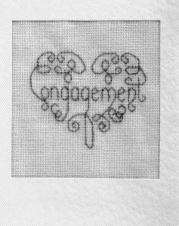

66

69

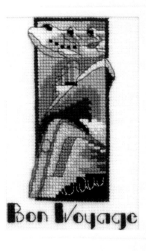

77

72

68

79

Happy New Job!

74

Happy Retirement

75

Congratulations Graduate!

71

On Your Wedding Day

67

New Home

76

You've Passed!

73

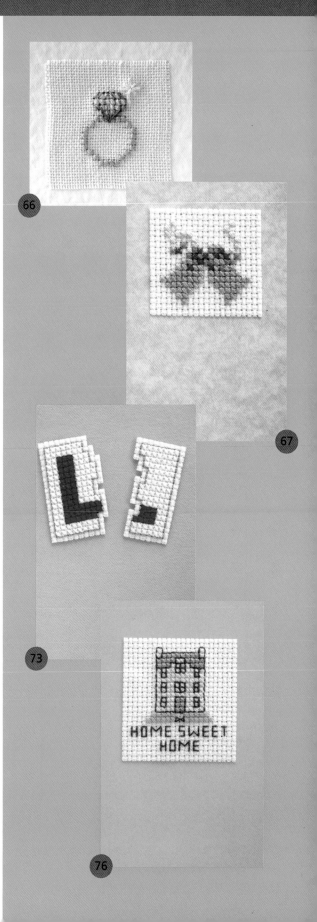

66

67

73

HOME SWEET HOME

76

Engagement

You will need
- 28 count cream evenweave 15 x 15cm (6 x 6in)

- DMC stranded cotton (floss) as listed in the key

- 152 x 104mm (6 x 4⅛in) card with 82 x 79mm (3¼ x 3⅛in) aperture – Craft Creations AP10U hammer cream

Note
Each stitch is worked over two threads of evenweave

Finished design size
5 x 6.5cm (2 x 2½in)

Quick to Stitch

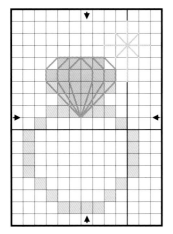

DMC stranded cotton

cross stitch
(use 2 strands) □ 676
backstitch
(use 1 strand) —— 318

DMC stranded metallic thread
cross stitch
(use 2 strands) ▨ 5272
backstitch
(use 2 strands) —— 5272

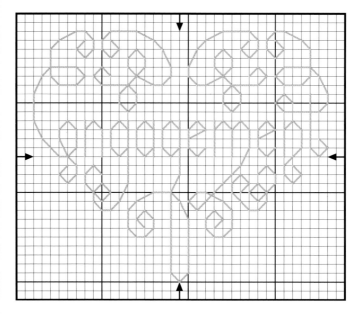

DMC stranded cotton
backstitch (use 1 strand)

—— 729

Wedding Roses

You will need

- 14 count white Aida
  20 x 20cm (8 x 8in)

- DMC stranded cotton
  (floss) as listed in the key

- 203 x 150mm (8 x 6in) card
  with 101 x 101mm (4 x 4in)
  aperture – Craft Creations
  AP04U hammer white

Finished design size
9.5 x 9.5cm (3¾ x 3¾in)

Quick to Stitch

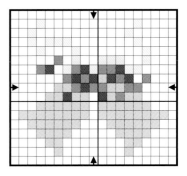

DMC stranded cotton
cross stitch (use 2 strands)

■	335
▨	415
□	963
▩	989

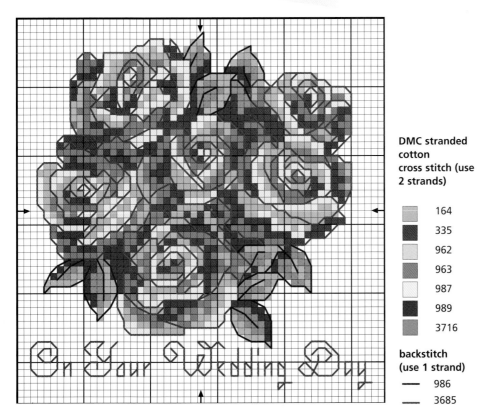

DMC stranded
cotton
cross stitch (use
2 strands)

▨	164
■	335
▨	962
▨	963
▨	987
■	989
▨	3716

backstitch
(use 1 strand)

—	986
—	3685

Wedding Cake

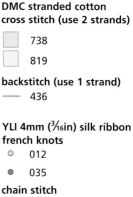

You will need

- 14 count white Aida 20 x 15cm (8 x 6in)

- DMC stranded cotton (floss) as listed in the key

- YLI 4mm (³⁄₁₆in) silk ribbon in light and dark cream as in the key

- 152 x 104mm (6 x 4⅛in) card with 114 x 70mm (4½ x 2¾in) aperture – Craft Creations AP08U hammer white

Finished design size

9.5 x 4.5cm (3¾ x 1¾in)

Note

Work the chain-stitch leaves with short – 26cm (10in) – lengths of ribbon and use a needle with an eye big enough to thread the ribbon through with no gathering. Bring the needle out of the hole at the end of the line closest to the French-knot roses. Without twisting the ribbon, work a chain stitch for each line on the chart (see Stitching Techniques, page 100). Keep the ribbon untwisted on the back. To begin, make a small knot in the end; to finish, weave the ribbon through a few stitches on the back

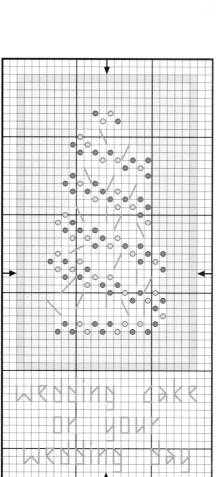

DMC stranded cotton cross stitch (use 2 strands)

▨	738
☐	819

backstitch (use 1 strand)

—— 436

YLI 4mm (³⁄₁₆in) silk ribbon french knots

○ 012
● 035

chain stitch

—— 012

Wedding Anniversary

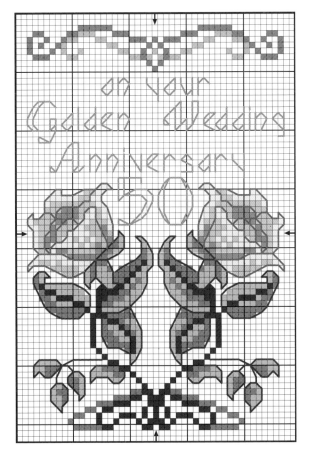

You will need

- 32 count antique white evenweave 20 x 18cm (8 x 7in)

- DMC stranded cotton (floss) as listed in the key

- 178 x 127mm (7 x 5in) card with 133 x 89mm (5¼ x 3½in) aperture – Impress Cards T42 ivory 1x

Note
Each stitch is worked over two threads of evenweave

Finished design size
11 x 7.5cm (4⅜ x 3in)

Golden wedding
Follow the colours in the key

Silver wedding
Work in the first alternative colours listed in the key for white roses with silver blue shading. Add 'Silver' and '25' in place of 'Golden' and '50', as charted on page 96

Ruby wedding
Work in the second alternative colours listed in the key for red roses. Add 'Ruby' and '40' in place of 'Golden' and '50', as charted on page 96

DMC stranded cotton cross stitch (use 2 strands)

▨	783 or 3325 or 816
▧	3345
▨	3347
▨	3348
▨	3820 or 3865 or 3801
☐	3822 or 775 or 321

backstitch (use 1 strand)

—	780 or 312 or 814
—	783 or 3325 or/ 816
—	3345

Anniversary Hearts

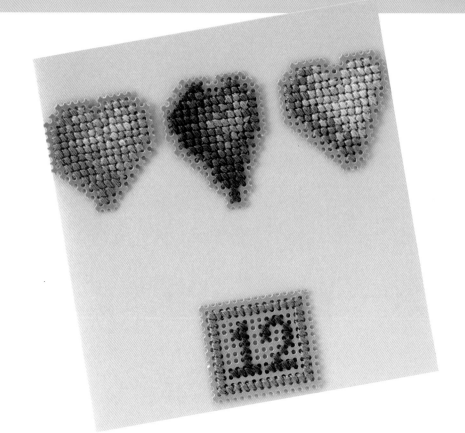

You will need

- 14 count silver perforated cross stitch paper 15 x 15cm (6 x 6in)

- DMC stranded cotton (floss) as listed in the key

- 100 x 100mm (4 x 4in) plain card – Craft Creations SF07U morphing mauve

- Double-sided tape

Finished design size

6.5 x 6.5cm (2½ x 2½in)

To personalize

Using three strands of 3807, stitch the number of the anniversary into the box, following the grey guidelines (see page 96). For a single figure, either add a nought in front or reduce the width of the box by five stitches

To finish

Draw round each shape on the back of the paper, leaving one row of paper on all sides. Trim the paper carefully with a pair of small, sharp scissors or a craft knife. Stick the designs onto the card using double-sided tape

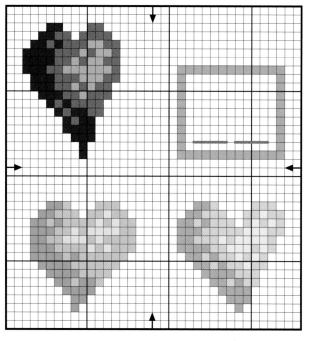

DMC stranded cotton cross stitch (use 3 strands)

	209
	210
	211
	603
	604
	605
	793
	794
	3807

Graduation

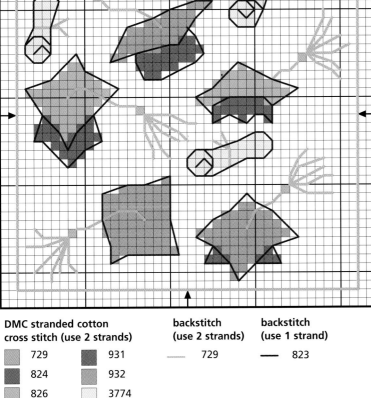

You will need

- 14 count cream Aida
  18 x 18cm (7 x 7in)

- DMC stranded cotton
  (floss) as listed in the key

- 152 x 104mm (6 x 4⅛in)
  card with 82 x 79mm
  (3¼ x 3⅛in) aperture – Craft
  Creations AP10U dark blue

- Gold pen

Finished design size
7.5 x 7.5cm (3 x 3in)

To finish
Using a gold pen, write
'Congratulations Graduate!'
or your own message below
the aperture

**DMC stranded cotton
cross stitch (use 2 strands)**

▨	729	
■	824	
▧	826	
▨	931	
▨	932	
▨	3774	

**backstitch
(use 2 strands)**

＝＝＝ 729

**backstitch
(use 1 strand)**

—— 823

Good Luck

You will need

- 28 count green evenweave 20 x 15cm (8 x 6in)

- DMC stranded cotton (floss) as listed in the key

- 178 x 114mm (7 x 4½in) plain card – Craft Creations SF02U lime green

- Double-sided tape

Note

Each stitch is worked over two threads of evenweave

Finished design size

9.5 x 3.5cm (3¾ x 1⅜in)

To finish

Trim the fabric to within 2cm (¾in) of the finished design. Fray the edges by carefully removing the outer row, then stick the design onto the card using double-sided tape

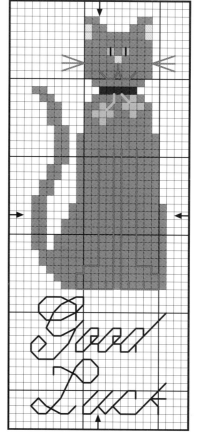

DMC stranded cotton cross stitch (use 2 strands)

	151
	310
	704
	825

backstitch (use 2 strands)
— 704

backstitch (use 1 strand)
— 310
— Blanc

You've Passed

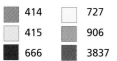

You will need

- 14 count cream Aida
  16 x 20cm (6¼ x 8in)

- DMC stranded cotton
  (floss) as listed in the key

- 156 x 111mm (6¼ x 4⅜in)
  card with 111 x 72mm
  (4⅜ x 2⅞in) aperture –
  Impress Cards T24
  sunflower 8x

Note

To make this into a
landscape card, cut 7mm
(¼in) off the bottom edge
(the margin here is wider
than at the top)

Finished design size

6.5 x 10.5cm (2½ x 4⅛in)

DMC stranded cotton cross stitch (use 2 strands)		backstitch (use 2 strands)	backstitch (use 1 strand)
414	727	— 632	— 336
415	906		
666	3837		

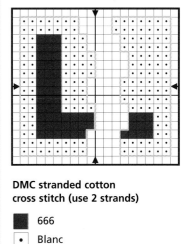

Quick to Stitch

DMC stranded cotton
cross stitch (use 2 strands)

■	666
·	Blanc

backstitch (use 2 strands)
— 318

New Job

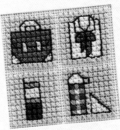

Happy New Job!

You will need
- 28 count cream evenweave 13 x 13cm (5 x 5in)

- DMC stranded cotton (floss) as listed in the key

- 114 x 88mm (4½ x 3½in) card with 40 x 40mm (1½ x 1½in) aperture – Craft Creations AP87U hammer cream

Note
Each stitch is worked over two threads of evenweave. Stitch either the male or female version of the card. (The same key is used for both.)

Finished design size
4 x 4cm (1½ x 1½in)

To finish
Write an appropriate message such as 'Good Luck In Your New Job' or 'Happy New Job!' below the aperture

Good Luck In Your New Job

DMC stranded cotton cross stitch (use 3 strands)

	211
	321
	407
	413
	415
	602
	604
	793
	3770
	3801
•	Blanc

backstitch (use 1 strand)
— 413

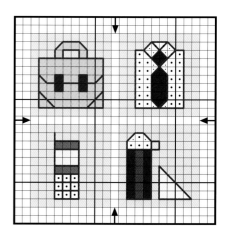

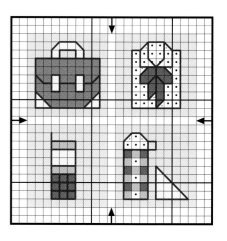

Sunny Retirement

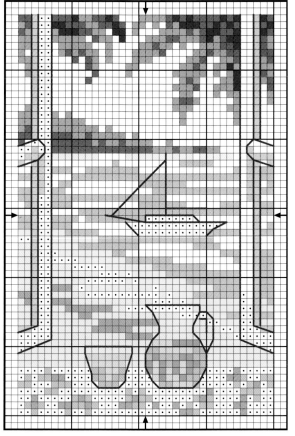

You will need

- 14 count blue Aida
  20 x 18cm (8 x 7in)

- DMC stranded cotton
  (floss) as listed in the key

- 152 x 104mm (6 x 4⅛in)
  plain card – Craft Creations
  SF03U pale yellow

- Double-sided tape

Finished design size

11 x 7cm (4⅜ x 2¾in)

To finish

Trim the fabric to within four
rows of Aida on all sides,
then fray the edges by
carefully removing the outer
row. Stick the design onto
the card using double-sided
tape. Write 'Happy
Retirement' underneath

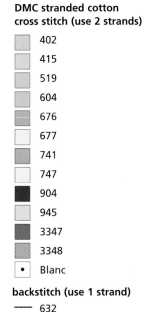

**DMC stranded cotton
cross stitch (use 2 strands)**

	402
	415
	519
	604
	676
	677
	741
	747
	904
	945
	3347
	3348
•	Blanc

backstitch (use 1 strand)

——	632

New Home

You will need

- 16 count cream Aida 18 x 18cm (7 x 7in)

- DMC stranded cotton (floss) as listed in the key

- 152 x 104mm (6 x 4⅛in) card with 82 x 79mm (3¼ x 3⅛in) aperture – Craft Creations AP10U hammer cream

Finished design size

8 x 8cm (3¼ x 3¼in)

Quick to Stitch

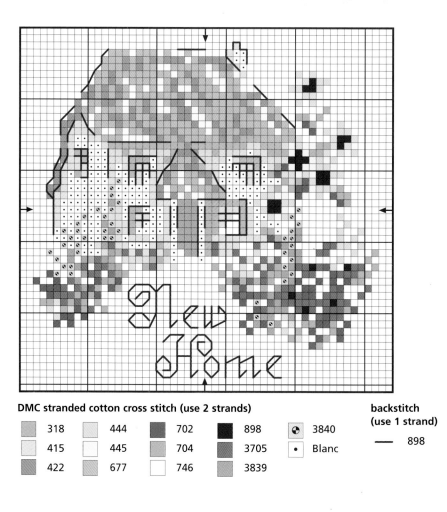

DMC stranded cotton cross stitch (use 2 strands)

318	444	702	898	3840	
415	445	704	3705	Blanc	
422	677	746	3839		

backstitch (use 1 strand)

—— 898

Bon Voyage

You will need

- 32 count antique white evenweave 20 x 18cm (8 x 7in)

- DMC stranded cotton (floss) as listed in the key

- 156 x 111mm (6¼ x 4⅜in) card with 111 x 72mm (4⅜ x 2⅞in) aperture – Impress Cards T24 ivory 1x

Note

Each stitch is worked over two threads of evenweave

Finished design size

11 x 7cm (4⅜ x 2¾in)

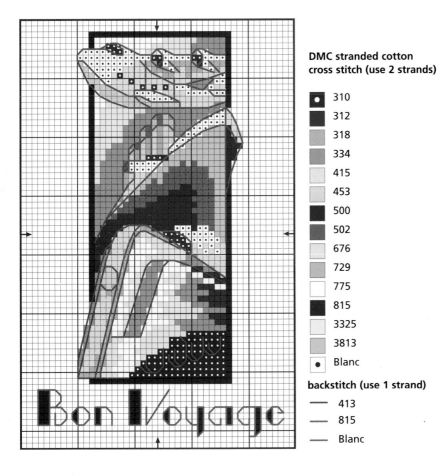

DMC stranded cotton cross stitch (use 2 strands)

◨	310
■	312
▨	318
▨	334
▨	415
▨	453
■	500
▨	502
▨	676
▨	729
□	775
■	815
▨	3325
▨	3813
•	Blanc

backstitch (use 1 strand)

—	413
—	815
—	Blanc

Thank You

You will need

- 16 count cream Aida
  18 x 20cm (7 x 8in)

- DMC stranded cotton
  (floss) as listed in the key

- 104 x 152mm (4⅛ x 6in)
  card with 70 x 114mm
  (2¾ x 4½in) aperture –
  Craft Creations AP08U
  dark blue

Finished design size

7 x 11cm (2¾ x 4⅜in)

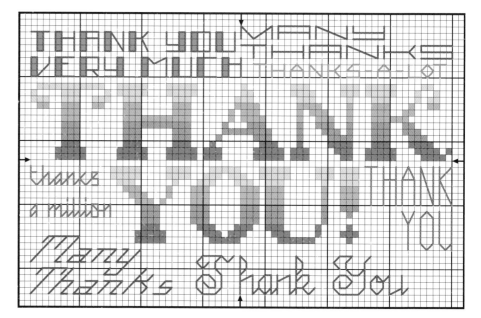

DMC stranded cotton
cross stitch (use 2 strands)

▨	165
▨	166
▨	581
▨	3819
▨	3833

backstitch (use 1 strand)

——	3607
——	3831
——	3833
——	3837

Thinking of You

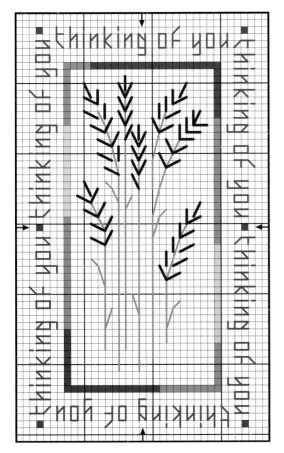

You will need

- 14 count white Aida
  20 x 18cm (8 x 7in)

- DMC stranded cotton
  (floss) as listed in the key

- 152 x 104mm (6 x 4⅛in)
  card with 114 x 70mm (4½
  x 2¾in) aperture – Craft
  Creations AP08U purple

Note

Chain stitch is used for the
lavender and is indicated on
the chart by a straight line.
Start your stitches at the end
of the line closest to the
green stems. For instructions
on working this stitch, see
page 100

Finished design size

10.5 x 6.5cm (4⅛ x 2½in)

DMC stranded cotton
cross stitch (use 2 strands)

- 210
- 340
- 3746

backstitch (use 1 strand)
— 3746
— 3817

chain stitch (use 2 strands)
— 340

Card Giver's Calendar

Quick to Stitch

Happy New Year

You will need

- 14 count cream Aida 20 x 15cm (8 x 6in)

- DMC stranded cotton (floss) as listed in the key

- 156 x 111mm (6¼ x 4⅜in) card with 111 x 72mm (4⅜ x 2⅞in) aperture – Impress Cards T24 gold linen 23

Finished design size

10 x 6.5cm (4 x 2½in)

Quick to Stitch

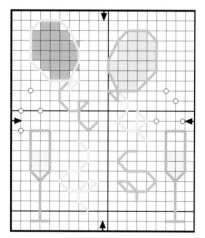

**DMC stranded cotton
cross stitch (use 2 strands)**

	164
	677
	3840

french knots (use 2 strands)
○ 677

backstitch (use 2 strands)
164
318
3840

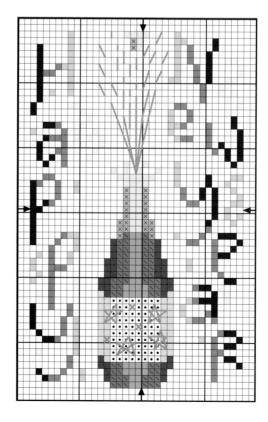

**DMC stranded cotton
cross stitch (use 2 strands)**

	472
	552
	553
	554
	676
	728
×	729
	762
\	910
	912
	3818
•	3865

Straight stitch (use 1 strand)
3829

Be My Valentine

You will need

- 14 count antique white Aida 18 x 15cm (7 x 6in)

- DMC stranded cotton (floss) and metallic thread as listed in the key

- Large-eyed needle for couching

- 118 x 91mm (4¾ x 3½in) card with 71 x 56mm (2¾ x 2¼in) aperture – Impress Cards T12 lilac felt 5x

Finished design size
7 x 5cm (2¾ x 2in)

Couching

Make a thread of six strands of gold thread. Using a needle with a large eye, bring the gold thread to the front of the work at point 'A'. Lay the gold thread loosely around the design. Secure it with small stitches of two strands of 915, worked around the gold thread at the points indicated, bringing the needle up and taking it down into the same hole. Alternatively, the line can be worked in backstitch using four strands of gold thread

**DMC stranded cotton
cross stitch (use 2 strands)**

■	915
▨	917
▧	3607

**DMC stranded metallic thread
for couching (use 6 strands)**

▬	5282

**DMC stranded cotton to secure the
couched thread (use 2 strands)**

⑊	915

**DMC stranded metallic thread
backstitch (use 2 strands)**

───	5282

Happy St Patrick's Day

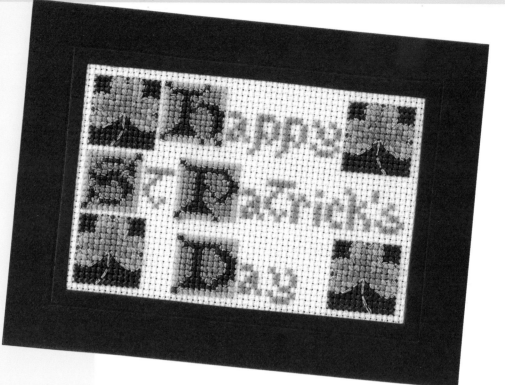

You will need

- 14 count cream Aida 15 x 20cm (6 x 8in)

- DMC stranded cotton (floss) and metallic thread as listed in the key

- 156 x 111mm (6¼ x 4⅜in) card with 111 x 72mm (4⅜ x 2⅞in) aperture – Impress Cards T24 pineleaf felt 4x

Note

To make this a landscape card, cut 7mm (¼in) off the bottom edge (the margin here is wider than at the top)

Finished design size

7 x 11cm (2¾ x 4⅜in)

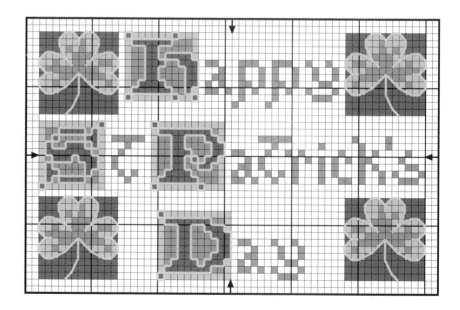

**DMC stranded cotton
cross stitch (use 2 strands)**

 906

907

986

**DMC stranded metallic thread
backstitch (use 2 strands)**

5282

Easter Bunny

You will need

- 14 count antique white Aida 23 x 18cm (9 x 7in)

- DMC stranded cotton (floss) as listed in the key

- 152 x 104mm (6 x 4⅛in) plain card – Craft Creations SF03U pale blue

Finished design size
11.5 x 7.5cm (4½ x 3in)

To finish
Trim the fabric to within four rows of Aida on all sides. Fray the edges by carefully removing the outer row. Stick the design onto the card using double-sided tape

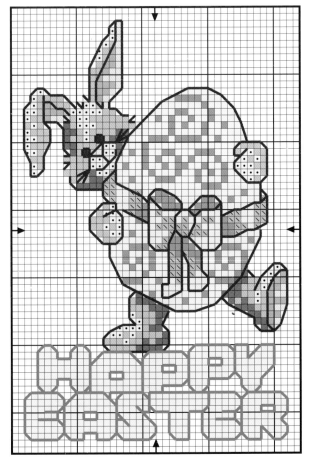

DMC stranded cotton cross stitch (use 2 strands)

▨	435
▨	437
•	739
■	801
☐	963
▨	3716
╲	3820
☐	3822
▨	3838
☐	3840
▨	3852

backstitch (use 1 strand)

—	801
—	3838

Quick to Stitch

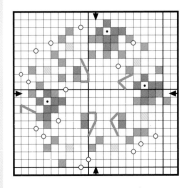

DMC stranded cotton cross stitch (use 2 strands)

▨	703	▨	3746
▨	725	•	Blanc
☐	727		

backstitch (use 2 strands)	french knots (use 2 strands)
— 703	○ Blanc

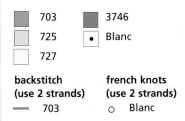

Easter Lilies

You will need

- 28 count cream evenweave 20 x 15cm (8 x 6in)

- DMC stranded cotton (floss) and metallic thread as listed in the key

- 156 x 111mm (6¼ x 4⅜in) card with 111 x 72mm (4⅜ x 2⅞in) aperture – Impress Cards T24 snow white linen 20

Finished design size
10 x 6.5cm (4 x 2½in)

Note
Each stitch is worked over two threads of evenweave

Alternative wording
Use 'He is Risen, Matthew 28:6' instead of 'Easter Blessings' (see page 96)

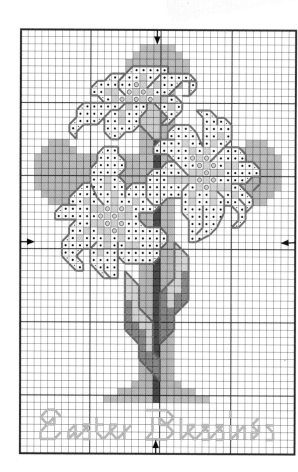

DMC stranded cotton cross stitch (use 2 strands)

▨	320
▨	367
▨	368
▨	453
•	Blanc

french knots (use 2 strands)

○ 3820

backstitch (use 1 strand)

—— 414

DMC stranded metallic thread cross stitch (use 2 strands)

▨ 5282

backstitch (use 2 strands)

〰〰 5282

Fourth of July

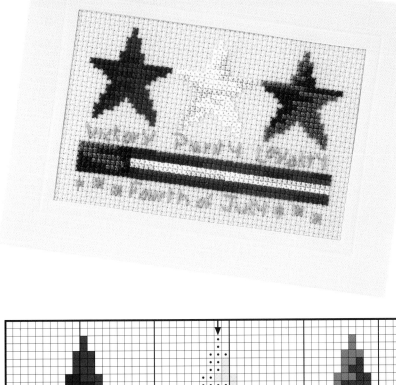

You will need

• 14 count ecru Aida
15 x 20cm (6 x 8in)

• DMC stranded cotton
(floss) as listed in the key

• 156 x 111mm (6¼ x 4⅜in)
card with 111 x 72mm
(4⅜ x 2⅞in) aperture –
Impress Cards T24
light cream linen 01

Note

To make this into a
landscape card, cut 7mm
(¼in) off the bottom edge
(the margin here is wider
than at the top)

Finished design size

6.5 x 10cm (2½ x 4in)

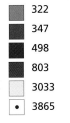

DMC stranded cotton
cross stitch (use 2 strands)

▨	322
▨	347
■	498
▨	803
▨	3033
•	3865

backstitch (use 2 strands)

━━━ 783

Rosh Hashanah

You will need

- 14 count cream Aida
  15 x 15cm (6 x 6in)

- DMC stranded cotton
  (floss) as listed in the key

- 127 x 127mm (5 x 5in)
  card with 76 x 76mm
  (3 x 3in) aperture –
  Impress Cards T33
  red linen 09

Finished design size

7 x 7cm (2¾ x 2¾in)

DMC stranded cotton
cross stitch (use 2 strands)

■	350
◪	351
▨	352
▨	353
▨	368
⊡	677
▨	728
▨	783
▨	3864

backstitch (use 2 strands)
▬ 632

backstitch (use 1 strand)
— 632

Diwali

You will need

- 14 count navy Aida
  18 x 18cm (7 x 7in)

- DMC stranded cotton
  (floss) as listed in the key

- 144 x 144mm (5⅝ x 5⅝in)
  plain card – Craft Creations
  SF06M pearly gold

- DMC metallic beads: pink
  (01 917), purple (05 333),
  orange (06 720) and
  gold (08 729)

Finished design size

10 x 10cm (4 x 4in)

To finish

Trim the fabric to within
three rows of Aida on all
sides. To attach the design to
the card, stitch a small cluster
of beads into one corner
using two strands of 915.
Place the design onto the
card and work a few stitches
through the centre bead and
through the fabric and card.
Fasten off the thread neatly
inside the card. Repeat for
the other corners

DMC stranded cotton
cross stitch (use 3 strands)

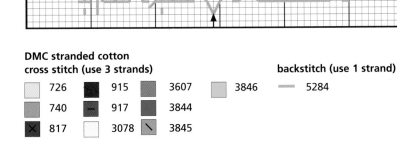

					backstitch (use 1 strand)
726	915	3607		3846	5284
740	917	3844			
817	3078	3845			

Hallowe'en

You will need

- 14 count navy Aida
  18 x 18cm (7 x 7in)

- DMC stranded cotton
  (floss) as listed in the key

- 152 x 152mm (6 x 6in)
  card with 101 x 101mm
  (4 x 4in) aperture –
  Impress Cards T48
  black linen 22

Finished design size
8.5 x 8.5cm (3⅜ x 3⅜in)

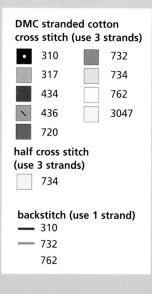

**DMC stranded cotton
cross stitch (use 3 strands)**

▨	310	▨	732
▨	317	▨	734
▨	434	▢	762
◪	436	▨	3047
▨	720		

**half cross stitch
(use 3 strands)**

▢	734

backstitch (use 1 strand)

——	310
——	732
	762

Thanksgiving

You will need

- 16 count cream Aida
  15 x 15cm (6 x 6in)

- DMC stranded cotton
  (floss) as listed in the key

- 127 x 127mm (5 x 5in) card
  with 76 x 76mm (3 x 3in)
  aperture – Impress Cards
  T33 light cream linen 01

Finished design size
7.5 x 7.5cm (3 x 3in)

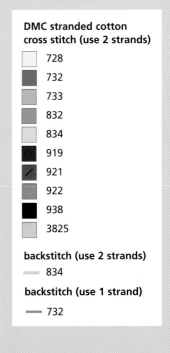

**DMC stranded cotton
cross stitch (use 2 strands)**

	728
	732
	733
	832
	834
	919
	921
	922
	938
	3825

backstitch (use 2 strands)
- 834

backstitch (use 1 strand)
— 732

Hanukkah

You will need

• 14 count navy blue Aida 18 x 20cm (7 x 8in)

• DMC stranded cotton (floss) and metallic thread as listed in the key

• 156 x 111mm (6¼ x 4⅜in) card with 111 x 72mm (4⅜ x 2⅞in) aperture – Impress Cards T24 cobalt felt 2x

Note

To make this into a landscape card, cut 7mm (¼in) off the bottom edge (the margin here is wider than at the top)

Finished design size

6.5 x 10cm (2½ x 4in)

Quick to Stitch:

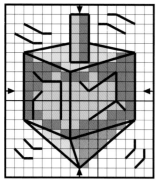

**DMC stranded cotton
cross stitch (use 2 strands)**

- 553
- 554
- 3839
- 3840

backstitch (use 2 strands)
— 3371

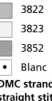

**DMC stranded cotton
cross stitch (use 2 strands)**

- 3822
- 3823
- 3852
- • Blanc

**DMC stranded metallic thread
straight stitch (use 2 strands)**
5282

Let it Snow!

You will need

- 28 count baby blue evenweave 20 x 18cm (8 x 7in)

- DMC stranded cotton as listed in the key

- 152 x 104mm (6 x 4⅛in) plain card – Craft Creations SF03U hammer white

- Double-sided tape

Finished design size
8 x 7cm (3⅛ x 2¾in)

Note
Each stitch is worked over two threads

To finish
Trim the fabric to within 2cm (¾in) of the finished design. Fold 1cm (½in) to the back and stitch neatly around all sides using 2 strands of 826. Use double-sided tape to attach the finished design to the card

DMC stranded cotton cross stitch (use 2 strands)

	754
	813
	826
	911
	913
	3777
•	Blanc

french knots (use 2 strands)

●	720
○	3852

backstitch (use 2 strands)

——	433
——	Blanc

backstitch (use 1 strand)

——	433

Christmas Tree

You will need

- 14 count ice blue Aida
  15 x 15cm (6 x 6in)

- DMC stranded cotton
  (floss) and metallic
  thread as listed in the key

- 90 x 90mm (3½ x 3½in)
  card with 54 x 54mm
  (2⅛ x 2⅛in) aperture –
  Impress Cards T16
  silver linen 25

Finished design size

5 x 5cm (2 x 2in)

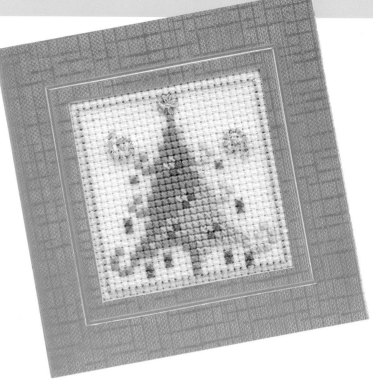

Quick to Stitch:

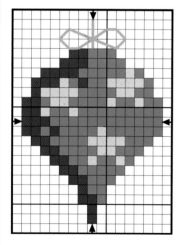

**DMC stranded cotton
cross stitch (use 2 strands)**

 158

793

5283 metallic

backstitch (use 2 strands)

5283 metallic

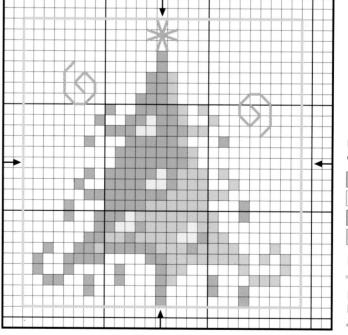

**DMC stranded cotton
cross stitch (use 2 strands)**

209

211

954

955

backstitch (use 2 strands)

157

**DMC metallic perlé 5
backstitch (use 1 strand)**

5283

Angel

You will need

- 14 count antique white Aida 23 x 20cm (9 x 8in)

- DMC stranded cotton (floss) and metallic thread as listed in the key

- 178 x 114mm (7 x 4½in) plain card – Craft Creations SF02U dark red (full card shown on page 81)

- 125 x 100mm (5 x 4in) gold card

Finished design size
12 x 9.5cm (4¾ x 3¾in)

To finish
Trim the fabric to within 2cm (¾in) of the finished design. Fold these turnings to the back and stitch down. Cut a piece of gold card 5mm (¼in) larger on all sides than the design. Using double-sided tape attach the design to the gold card, then attach the gold card to the red card

DMC stranded cotton cross stitch (use 2 strands)

■	300
╱	347
▮	400
▮	402
×	422
>	676
	677
—	680
•	712
	754
↖	758
■	796
⊙	814
◣	816
■	922
◨	938
╱	945
	948
○	951
⌐	3826
	5282 metallic

backstitch (use 1 strand)

— 356

Letters, Words and Numbers

If you like a card but the sentiment is wrong for your needs, use the alphabets, words, phrases and numbers on the following pages to personalize the card. You could include the recipient's name, age or a message of your own.

Christening Lamb, page 12

Magical Birthday, page 24

Alien Birthday, page 25

Football Pennant, page 30

First Holy Communion, page 32

Anniversary Hearts, page 70

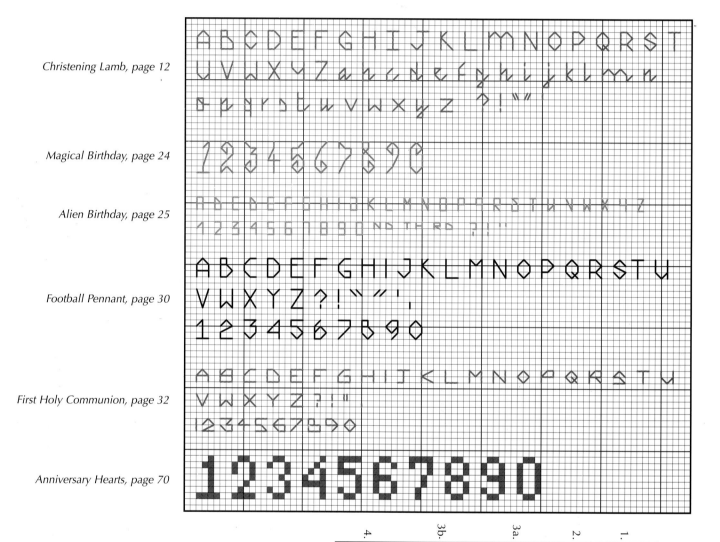

1. For New Grandparents, page 14

2. Bar Mitzvah, page 33

3a & 3b. Wedding Anniversary, page 69

4. Easter Lilies, page 86

Words for Her

This alphabet and the word sets are designed for use with the women's cards on pages 34–49, but they can be used for any card in this book.

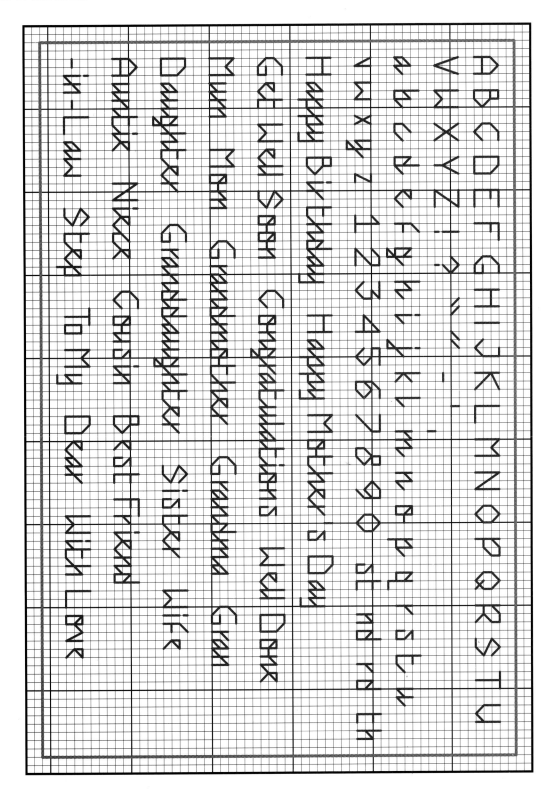

Words for Him

Use this alphabet and the word sets with the men's cards on pages 50–63, or apply them to any other card in this book for a personal touch.

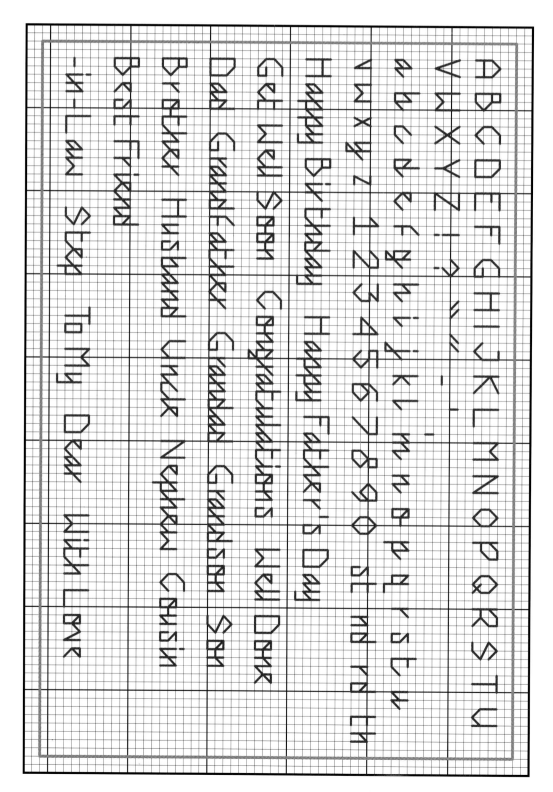

Stitching Techniques

One of the joys of this book is that you don't need a lot of time or an extensive stitching repertoire to produce wonderful results. Only a few stitches are used and they are all clearly explained and illustrated here.

Getting started

To begin stitching, find the centre of your fabric by folding in half and then half again. Arrows at the edges mark the centre lines of each chart. Match these to the fold lines on your fabric, and start stitching where they cross. Do not use a knot to secure your thread. Instead take the thread down through the fabric about 2.5cm (1in) from your starting point and work the first few stitches over this tail to anchor it; trim off the excess. To finish a thread, weave it through the back of a few stitches.

Working cross stitch

Cross stitch Each full coloured square on the chart represents one cross stitch on the fabric. Cross stitch can be worked singly or as a row of stitches when there is a block of the same colour, as demonstrated here. Make sure that the top diagonal of each stitch lies in the same direction, from bottom right to top left.

Cross stitch on Aida

Cross stitch on evenweave

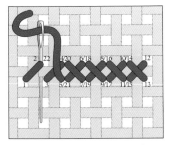

Row of cross stitches on Aida

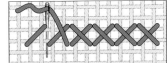

Row of cross stitches on evenweave (use the same stitching sequence as shown left)

Quarter and three-quarter stitches Partial coloured squares on the chart represent quarter or three-quarter stitches, which help to smooth out the lines of a design. A quarter stitch is simply a short diagonal stitch taken to the centre of the block of Aida (or between the threads of evenweave fabric), while a three-quarter stitch is the first half of a cross stitch plus a quarter stitch. The diagrams below show how these are worked. When using Aida you must pierce the centre of a block to complete these stitches. Either change to a sharp sewing needle for this purpose or use a bodkin or other pointed object to make a hole through which you can pass your tapestry needle.

Quarter stitch (white) and three-quarter stitch (blue) on evenweave

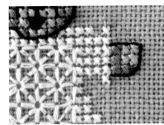

Three-quarter cross stitches on Aida

Pulled cross stitch For this stitch simply pull each cross stitch tightly to draw the fabric threads together, forming a pattern of holes. This provides attractive detailing on the arms of the robe featured in the 'Christening Teddy' card on page 13.

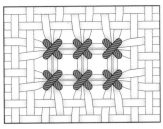

Christening Teddy, page 13

Working additional stitches

Other stitches needed to complete all the cards in this book are backstitch, straight stitch, French knots, chain stitch and couching, which are all clearly demonstrated here.

Backstitch is ideal for adding fine details to a design or for working the wording of a card. It is also useful for strengthening the outline of a shape. Bring the needle up, take it back one stitch length and then bring it up one stitch length beyond your starting point, as shown.

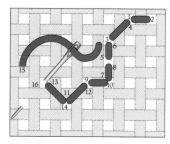

Cricket, page 59

Straight stitch is simply a long stitch worked in a straight line. It is used to add linear details as on 'Eighteen' (page 40). Bring the needle up at the start of the stitch and then take it down at the finish, pulling the thread so that it lies flat against the fabric.

French knot is a well-known textured stitch that can be worked singly or in clusters, which is widely used in this book. If the symbol in the chart is on the line, as in 'Wedding Cake' (page 68), bring the needle up in the hole to the right of the symbol, wrap the thread once or twice around the needle and then pass the needle through the hole directly to the left. If the symbol is in the middle of a square, work the stitch by bringing the needle up at the top right, wrapping the thread around the needle, and taking it down at the bottom left. Pull tightly to produce a neat knot on the surface.

Chain stitch is used to work ribbon details on the 'Wedding Cake' card (page 68) and for the lavender flowers on the 'Thinking of You' card (page 79). Simply bring the needle out of the hole at the starting point, wrap the thread/ribbon loosely around the needle and push it back into the same hole, then bring it out at the finishing point, catching the loop. Pull the thread/ribbon gently to form a chain stitch and then take the needle back down into the same hole to anchor the stitch.

Thinking of You, page 79

Couching produces a bold outline and enables you to use a thicker or more embellished thread than normal (see 'Be My Valentine' on page 83). Using a needle with a large eye, bring the thicker thread to the front of the work and lay it loosely in place around the design. Secure it with small stitches, using a thinner thread, worked around the thick thread at the points indicated on the chart. Bring the needle up and take it down into the same hole each time.

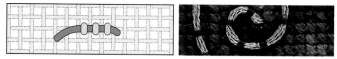

Be My Valentine, page 83

Wedding Cake, page 68 (includes french knots and chain stitch worked in ribbon)

Eyelets These are used on the 'Christening Teddy' card shown on page 13 to give the front of the Christening robe an attractive lacy look. Simply work a series of long stitches into the same hole, as shown.

Christening Teddy, page 13

Using beads

For additional texture, colour and sparkle, some of the cards in this book are embellished with beads. These are attached as part of a cross stitch. Thread the bead onto the needle while working the first part of the cross, and then complete the cross by laying one strand each side of the bead, as shown in the diagram below.

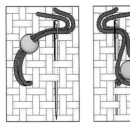
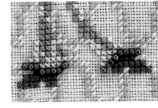

Babe, page 26

Working with waste canvas

Waste canvas enables you to work regular cross stitches on any fabric, as on the '18th Birthday' surfboard card on page 55. First tack the waste canvas securely into position on the fabric so that it does not move while you are working. Using a sharp needle, stitch through the waste canvas and the fabric behind, pushing the needle through the small holes to keep the stitches looking neat. When the stitching is finished, trim away the excess canvas and dampen it slightly. Remove the threads of the canvas one by one, taking care not to pull the cross stitches out of shape as you do so.

Making a twisted cord

The 'Football Pennant' on page 30 uses a cord made from twisted thread. To make a twisted cord first take two strands of perlé thread and measure off three times the length of cord required. Knot a loop at each end. Place one loop over a hook or door handle and insert a pencil into the other loop. Stand away from the attached end so that the threads are taut and begin twisting the pencil. Keep twisting until the cord starts to curl. The tighter you twist, the firmer the cord will be. Carefully bring the two ends together, holding onto the centre of the cord. Let the cord twist together. Knot each end to stop the cord untwisting, but leave the ends free to form small tassels.

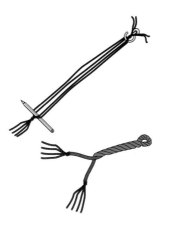

Football Pennant, page 30

Working a knotted-in fringe

The 'Football Pennant' (page 30) also has a knotted-in fringe. To make this, cut a length of cardboard 4cm (1½in) wide. Wind perlé thread around it neatly and cut along one side to produce threads of equal length. Fold one length in half and thread both ends onto a large-eyed needle. Push the needle through the edge of the fabric from front to back, pulling the loop through. Remove the needle and pass the ends through the loop. Pull gently to tighten. Place the next loop close to this one and continue around the fabric. Using a sharp pair of scissors, trim the fringe neatly, if necessary.

Finishing Your Card

If you have made one of the Quick to Stitch projects you can probably mount it straight away. You won't have handled it much so it should be clean. A larger design for a card may have picked up a little dirt and in that case you should wash it gently in warm water with a non-biological powder. Most good threads are colourfast, but do check first if in doubt. Do not wring the work to get rid of water but roll it in a towel to blot off as much as possible. Cover your ironing board with a towel and press the work on the wrong side; the towel prevents the stitches from being flattened. Iron it until dry.

Now you are ready to mount the work. How you do this depends on the type of card you have chosen – with or without an aperture. Both types of card are easy to use once you have the hang of it, but do take care with this stage because the presentation is so important.

Using a card with a ready-made aperture

Aperture cards have three sections. Your stitched piece is mounted behind the middle section, which contains the aperture. One of the other two sections folds over to cover the stitching and the remaining section forms the back of the card. Sometimes the aperture is cut high in the card to allow room for a message to be written beneath it. Mark the top of the card on the inside to ensure that you put the stitching in the right way up.

1. Lay the card right side up on top of the design so the stitching is in the middle of the aperture. Place a pin in each corner and remove the card. Trim the fabric to within about 15mm (½in) so it fits inside the card.

Happy New Job!

2. On the wrong side of the card, stick double-sided tape around the aperture and peel off the backing tape.

3. Place the card over the design, using the pins to guide it into position. Press down firmly so the fabric is stuck securely to the card.

4. On the wrong side of the card, stick more double-sided tape around the edge of the middle section and peel off the backing tape. Fold in the left section to cover the back of the stitching and press down firmly. Fold in the right section to finish.

Making your own aperture card

All the cards used in this book are available ready-made but you may prefer to make your own, which allows you greater control over the colour and texture of the card and over the shape of the aperture.

You will need
- Sheet of card
- Sheet of paper
- Sharp scissors or a craft knife
- Pencil and ruler

1. Measure the finished size of the stitching and decide on the shape of the aperture. Draw this shape onto a piece of paper and cut out carefully. Check that the aperture is big enough to fit around the stitching.

2. Allowing margins of at least 2cm (¾in), draw a rectangle or a square around the aperture, making sure the corners are right angles. This will be the size of the finished card. Place it on your stitching to make sure the finished card is the correct size. Sometimes a large design needs a larger margin of card around it to look balanced. Refer to the photographs of finished cards in this book for ideas.

3. Place this paper template onto the wrong side of a piece of card, matching the bottom edges, and lightly draw around the outside edge of the template with a pencil. Move the template along and draw another card shape next to the first. Repeat once more until you have a long rectangle of three sections. Score gently along each line between the sections with the back of a craft knife to make folding easier. Cut out the rectangle.

4. Place the template into the centre section and draw carefully around the aperture shape.

5. Cut out the aperture with a craft knife, carefully cutting into the corners. Trim the left edge of the first section by about 2mm (¹⁄₁₆in) so it lies flat when folded over to the inside of the card. This will cover the back of the stitching.

6. Fold in the left and then the right section along the scored lines.

7. Mount your stitching following the instructions on the left for a card with a ready-made aperture.

Using a plain card

A plain card has no aperture but it may have an embossed 'frame' around the edges. The stitched piece should be attached centrally to the front. Use double-sided tape because glue is likely to seep through the fabric, ruining your hard work. Double-sided tape is also quick and efficient, making this the ideal mounting option for your Quick to Stitch projects.

1. Measure the card and decide how much of a border you would like to leave around the stitched fabric. If the card has an embossed frame, measure the area inside the frame; you will need to trim the fabric to fit neatly.

2. Trim the edges of the fabric carefully with a sharp pair of scissors, following the line of one of the threads. There should be an equal border of fabric all around the stitched design. If you wish, fray the edges by removing the outer row of Aida or a few threads of evenweave fabric.

3. Turn the design over and carefully stick double-sided tape around the edges. Peel off the backing tape and then press the fabric firmly in position on the front of the card.

The Quick to Stitch designs featured throughout the book are small enough to be used as gift tags. Stitch them and then simply stick onto a ready-made tag with double-sided tape. They can also make a really quick card; mount them into an aperture card or stick onto a larger plain card and add your own message.

Adding a message

Many of the cards have a hand-written message. You can write this freehand or use dry transfer lettering or gold label stickers. Alternatively, if you have a computer, type your message using a clear font and the correct size to fit onto the card. Print it out and either cut round the message and stick this label onto the card or trace over the writing using a soft pencil. To transfer this to the card first scribble over the back of the tracing paper with the pencil, then place the tracing right side up over the card. Write over the message but do not press too hard. The pencil lines should be faint as a guide only. Write carefully over the pencil lines using a metallic or ink pen. Or why not stitch a greeting using the letters, words and numbers charts on pages 96-98.

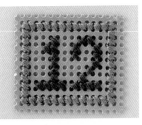

Conversion Chart

All the cards in this book are worked in DMC threads. If you can't obtain these or prefer the Anchor brand, use this chart as a guide to substitutions. An Asterisk indicates that a colour has been used more than once; it may be duplicated in a design.

DMC	Anchor	DMC	Anchor	DMC	Anchor	DMC	Anchor	DMC	Anchor
B5200	1	368	214	712	926	825	162	3340	329
Blanc	2*	369	1043	718	88	826	161*	3345	268
150	59*	400	351	720	326	828	9159	3347	266
151	73	402	1047	721	324	832	907	3348	264
154	873	407	914	722	323*	834	874	3364	261
157	120*	413	236	725	305*	838	1088	3371	382
158	178	414	235*	726	295*	840	1084	3607	87
161	176*	415	398	727	293	894	26	3608	86
162	159*	422	372	728	305*	898	380	3685	1028
163	877*	433	358	729	890	902	897*	3687	68
164	240	434	310	732	281*	904	258	3688	75*
165	278*	435	365	733	280*	905	257	3689	49
166	280*	436	363	734	279	906	256*	3705	35*
208	110	437	362	739	366	907	255	3716	25
209	109	444	291	740	316	910	230	3733	75*
210	108	445	288	741	304	911	205	3746	1030
211	342	453	231	743	302	912	209	3747	120*
221	897*	472	253	744	301	913	204	3752	1032
223	895	498	1005	745	300	915	1029	3770	1009
224	893	500	683	746	275	917	89	3772	1007
300	352	502	877*	747	158	919	340	3774	778
304	19	519	1038	754	1012	921	1003*	3777	1015
310	403	550	101	758	9575	922	1003*	3801	1098
312	979	552	99	762	234	931	1034	3806	62*
317	400	553	98*	772	259	932	1033	3807	122
318	235*	554	95	775	128	938	381	3813	875*
319	1044	562	210	780	309	939	152*	3816	876
320	215	564	206	783	307	945	881	3817	875*
321	47	581	281*	792	941	946	332	3818	923
322	978	600	59*	793	176*	948	1011	3819	278*
334	977	602	57	794	175	951	1010	3820	306*
335	40	603	62*	796	133	954	203*	3822	295*
336	150	604	55	797	132	955	203*	3823	386
340	118	605	1094	798	146	959	186*	3825	323*
341	117*	606	334	799	145	961	76	3826	1049
347	1025	632	936	801	359	962	75*	3829	901*
349	13*	666	46	803	149	963	23	3831	29
350	11	676	891	813	161*	964	185	3833	31*
351	10	677	361	814	45	970	925	3835	98*
352	9	680	901*	815	44	986	246	3837	100*
353	8	701	227	816	43	987	244	3838	177
355	1014	702	226	817	13*	989	242	3839	176*
356	1013	703	238	823	152*	996	433	3840	117*
367	216	704	256*	824	164	3033	387	3841	159*
						3046	887	3844	410
						3047	852	3845	1089*
						3051	845	3846	1090
						3052	844	3852	306*
						3064	883	3853	1003*
						3078	292	3864	376
						3325	129	3865	2*

SUPPLIERS

INDEX

Suppliers

The threads, fabrics and cards used in this book are widely available in needlecraft shops and department stores. To find a stockist near you, contact the following companies:

Stranded cotton, Zweigart Aida and evenweave linen
DMC
UK: DMC Creative World Ltd, Pullman Road, Wigston, Leicester, LE18 2DY
tel: 0116 281 1040

USA: The DMC Corporation, Port Kearney Bld, 10 South Kearney, New Jersey 070732 0650
tel: 201 589 0606

Australia: DMC Needlecraft Pty Ltd, PO Box 317, Earlswood 2206, New South Wales 2204
tel: 2 559 3088

Cards
Impress Cards & Craft Materials
Slough Farm, Westhall, Suffolk, IP19 8RN
tel: 01986 781422
email: sales@impresscards.co.uk
www.impresscards.com

Craft Creations Ltd
Ingersoll House, Delamare Road, Cheshunt, Hertfordshire, EN8 9HD
tel: 01992 781900
email: enquiries@craftcreations.com
www.craftcreations.com

Beads
Mill Hill Inc
UK: Groves & Banks, Drakes Drive Industrial Estate, Long Crendon, Aylesbury, Bucks, HP18 9BA
tel: 01844 258100
email: info@groves-banks.com
www.groves-banks.com

USA: Gay Bowles Sales Inc, PO Box 1060, Janesville, WI 53545
website: www.millhill.com

Ribbon
YLI Corporation
UK: Quilt Direct, Pym Street, Tavistock, Devon, PL19 0AW
tel: 0500 418083
email: enquiries@quiltdirect.co.uk
www.quiltdirect.com

USA: 161, West Main Street, Rock Hill, SC 29730
tel: 803-985-3100
email: ylicorp@ylicorp.com
www.ylicorp.com

HAPPY 4TH
BIRTHDAY
EARTH BOY

BIRTHDAY BOY
21

snails & puppydog tails

Happy
Birthday

May sweetness fill

your new year

stitching now —
housework never

Happy Retirement